Be the Captain of Your Career

a new approach to career planning and advancement

by

Jack Molisani

published by

PRECISION
WORDAGE
PRESS

Pasadena, CA

Published by **Precision Wordage Press**
a division of Precision Wordage Inc
PO Box 94536
Pasadena, CA 91109

Published in the United States of America
First Printing May 2014

Trade paperback
ISBN 978-0-9627090-2-9

eBook
ISBN 972-0-9627090-9-8

Kindle
ISBN 978-1-940632-01-8

PDF
ISBN 978-1-940632-00-1

Excerpts from this book were previously published in *Intercom* magazine.

Practical Information That Works!

"As I was listening to your presentations on resumes, interviewing, and portfolios, I had a feeling that I was getting wonderful advice. Now I KNOW I got great advice. Your presentations gave me some really good tips and those changes were a key factor in my getting the position.

– MK Grueneberg, Chicago, IL

"Because of you, I just received an offer for a permanent job that I think I am going to love. Your advice was invaluable. I just wanted to let you know what a difference you made and how grateful I am."

– J. Hamrick, Austin, TX

"To get the job of your dreams and succeed in your chosen career, look no further than this book. Molisani has written a terrific, no-nonsense guide full of great advice and smart tips, from resumes, to interviewing, to landing and succeeding in that great job. Filled with entertaining stories, it's a fun read, too. Bravo!"

– Chellie Campbell, author of *The Wealthy Spirit*

"Whether you are a new graduate or career changer, Jack's challenge to be the captain of your career will motivate you. Read the book, follow his tips, and you'll have the career of your dreams."

– Victoria Koster-Lenhardt, Global Employment Advisor
European Region, U.S. Department of State

"In this straight-talking, insightful book, Jack tells you what you how to create a career you love. His wisdom, gained from years as a top recruiter, will guide you in a positive, clear direction. Whether you are a new job seeker or an experienced candidate, I highly recommend Jack's book to steer your career the right way."

– Pamela Paterson, author of
Get the Job: Optimize Your Resume for the Online Job Search

Introduction

Do you feel that you are the captain of your career, going exactly where you want to go, when you want, and the way you want?

Or do you feel more like a galley slave chained to a job you hate, perhaps one that pays slave wages?

This book is about creating the standard of living you've always wanted—even if you think that goal is unattainable.

If you picked up this book then I bet you feel just like I did early in my career:

- You know what you want and where you want to be.
- You're just not sure how to get there.

Does any of this strike a chord?

If so, this book is for you.

Keep Me Posted

Consider this not just a book, but more like a conversation between us: I'll share some career- and life-changing realizations I've made over the decades, and you'll let me know how you're doing applying these lessons in your own life.

Keep me posted on your successes and challenges, new outlooks on life, and new prosperity achieved!

Email me at *Jack@BeTheCaptainOfYourCareer.com,* or follow me on Twitter *@JackMolisani.*

Contents

Section 3: HAVE IT
How to Get What
You Really Want in Life

Section I: THINK IT
How to Get Your Career Moving
In the Right Direction

The first section of this book is about change.

I am a firm believer that you not only choose the path you want in life, you *create* the path you walk in life.

Not happy with your current path? Create a new one!

Here's how.

The First Thing to Do When You Find Yourself in a Hole: Stop Digging

One of the things I do to make money is IT staffing—a "headhunter" for engineers, project managers, technical writers, etc. In fact, I have owned my own staffing agency for years.

My company (like many) was hit hard in the economic crash of 2008. As a headhunting agency, we only get paid when our clients hire our candidates. And in the blink of an eye, our number of jobs to fill went from 123 to 0.

Zero.

And while the company's gross income went from $1.8 million a year to practically nothing overnight, I still had employees to pay, contracts I couldn't break, lines of credit I used to cover the bills when clients were late paying me, etc. Many of my employees were literally my friends, so I didn't want to lay them off. Plus, I (mistakenly) thought that the hiring freeze was only going to last a month or two.

So I started borrowing money to cover payroll, pay the rent, pay the bills.

I burned through my savings, then my lines of credit. I borrowed from friends, from my parents, from associates. I even went as far as to use funds that were earmarked for subcontractors to pay other bills, leaving me unable to pay the subs when their invoices were due. I was digging myself deeper and deeper in debt and knew if I didn't stop, I'd pass the point of no return, if I hadn't already.

So I stopped, did an honest assessment of the mess I'd made, then started to put things right.

I told my employees that if they didn't find jobs to fill, I wouldn't be able to pay them. They couldn't, so I finally let them go.

I then confronted just how deep in debt I was: $480,000.

Next, I took the brutally painful (but equally necessary) step of calling all the subcontractors to whom I owed money and confessed that I had spent the money meant for them. I promised I'd pay them back every dime I owed them—plus interest—but they had to give me time to turn things around.

I then called my other creditors and let them know I was dangerously close to bankruptcy, and I was offering them a choice: they could either work with me and reduce the payment terms, or I'd be forced to declare bankruptcy and they'd get nothing.

Fortunately they all agreed to modify my payment terms, and I was able to avoid bankruptcy.

So I found a technical writing contract I could do myself (one of the jobs I've had in the past), put myself on a super austerity budget, and got to work rebuilding the staffing business.

It took years of hard work, tight belts, and giving hand-made presents to family at Christmas. But I made it.

So can you.

There is more I learned from this time period that I'll share later in the book, but for now take away these two important lessons:

- The first thing you should do when you find yourself in a hole is *stop digging*.
- No matter how bad things are, you *can* make things right.

Stay Positive

I've observed over the years that fear of losing one's job is a deep and powerful emotion—even more so for those who have families to support. I've also noticed there are those who would prey on that fear for their own advantage, such as the media to get ratings and politicians to get votes.

It seems like there is always a reason to be fearful: economic recessions, threats of war, continued unrest in the Middle East (which is probably done on purpose to prop up world oil prices).

So the first bit of advice I would share with those concerned about their jobs is this:

Stay positive.

Why?

Because you can't fix what you believe you can't control.

In other words, if you think finding a good job in this economy is hopeless, you might as well just sit at home all day watching TV, as nothing you do will matter anyway. Ditto for "we're heading into a recession," as that is a classic example of a self-fulfilling prophecy. If enough companies stop hiring and begin laying off workers out of fear of a recession, their actions end up causing the very condition they feared would occur!

So what's a person in need of a job (or a better job) to do?

First, stop thinking like a victim (if you have been) and realize that no matter how bad things seem, no matter how bad the media says things are, there are actions you can take *right here and right now* to increase your standard of living.

Let's look at a few.

Never Lose Faith

In the book *Good to Great: Why Some Companies Make the Leap and Others Don't*, a team of researchers identified how some companies made the leap from bad to great, while other companies (when faced with similar challenges) didn't.

The companies who went from bad to great (sustainably great, not just a momentary surge) had several aspects in common.

The researchers named one of the traits that all the companies shared "The Stockdale Paradox" after Admiral Stockdale, who, despite being tortured for eight years in a prisoner-of-war camp during the Vietnam War, never gave up, never lost faith.

> *"I never lost faith in the end of the story. I never doubted not only that I would get out, but also that I would prevail in the end and turn the experience into the defining event of my life, which, in retrospect, I would not trade.*
>
> *"This is a very important lesson. You must never confuse faith that you will prevail in the end—which you can never afford to lose—with the discipline to confront the most brutal facts of your current reality, whatever they might be."*

I never lost faith that I would prevail in the end regardless of the difficulties, *and*, at the same time, I confronted the most brutal facts of the reality I was in.

Then I did what I had to do to make it right.

I did it.

So can you.

Seven Career Lessons I Learned from Selling Ginsu Knives

2008 wasn't the first time my life and career came crashing down. In the mid 1990s, I was laid off from my full-time job as a sales engineer with a bank technology company.

I spent months looking for a new engineering position, but no one was hiring.

At the time, a friend owned a franchise to place booths selling Ginsu® knives into home and garden shows. One of her regular salespersons had to go out of town and she asked if I could cover. I thought, why not? I could use the money.

They gave me a crash course in how to demonstrate Ginsu knives and sent me off to work a show. I did well—so well they invited me to work the whole home and garden show circuit. So I put my stuff in storage, leased a cargo van, and traveled the country for a year selling Ginsu knives.

At the end of that year the economy had begun to recover but I still couldn't find work as a sales engineer. I *was* able to find work as a technical writer—a job I found I was good at and very much enjoyed.

It has been fifteen years since I traveled the country working the home and garden show circuit, but I will always remember seven career lessons I learned from selling Ginsu knives:

1. **Have a good product to sell.**

   Yes, Ginsu knives really can cut a hammer and then slice a tomato paper thin. To this day I still have a Ginsu knife in my kitchen for cutting bread, and one in the car for cutting radiator hoses. The product really works!

   The lesson: Find a product or service that really works and sell it. (Or deliver it if someone else in your organization sells it.)

2. **Stand behind your product.**

   Ginsu knives rarely get dull or break, but it does happen (especially when you use one to saw down a small tree). The knife's lifetime guarantee says you can mail it back to the manufacturer or present the knife to any salesperson in the world and they will replace it for free, no questions asked. And they do!

   The lesson: Stand behind your product and guarantee its quality.

3. **Attract positive attention.**

   In pitchman lingo, your "tip" is the crowd that gathers to watch you demonstrate your product. The bigger the tip, the more people who will buy—not just in number of sales, but also in percentage of closes (more on this later).

   Most people tend to ignore salespeople (or worse, go out of their way to avoid them). People rarely walk up to a booth to see what you are selling. You have to attract their attention, call them over, be entertaining, be interesting.

   The lesson: Similarly, customers rarely call to buy your product or service. *You* have to find *them*. Use social media, live webinars, direct mail, anything you can think of to attract positive attention from your target audiences.

4. **The closer your "tip" is to your "joint," the more sales you will make.**

As I said earlier, your "tip" is the group standing around your booth watching your sales pitch (or hanging around waiting for you to start if you work the room properly). Your "joint" is the booth from which you are demonstrating your product.

The closer people are to your joint, the more likely they are to buy. Most people, however, will stop about ten feet away, cross their arms defensively, and watch from afar (interested, but too timid to get closer).

I'll let you in on a secret: Pitchmen know people are hesitant to walk up to salespeople, so to get people to move closer (and thus more likely to buy), a pitchman might say, "Now I'm going to show how the knife really can cut a hammer, but the people in the back are going to have to move forward to see the shavings."

The pitchman will then take three steps backwards to make a comfortable space for the audience to move into as he motions them forward. But then, once everyone has moved closer, the pitchman will take three steps forward again and be right there nose-to-nose with the tip, then continue the demonstration.

The lesson: People can't confront a sales pitch right from the start, so have a way to get them involved first. Offer a free webinar, a podcast, a low-cost intro service, etc. Then continue your main presentation—and land more clients.

5. **Ask for the sale.**

As a pitchman you can do the most beautiful demonstration in the world, but if you end it with, "Well there you go. Thanks for watching!", people will just smile and walk away empty-handed. But if you ask for the sale, you'll get some.

Or better yet, assume they are going to buy and just direct them to your helper (see point #6). And once someone buys, others will as well. (Call it herd mentality, breaking the ice, or safety in numbers. Most people just hate to go first.)

The lesson: You have to ask for the sale. The same holds true when asking to close a deal or asking your employer for a raise—you have to *ask*.

6. Get a helper.

People hate to wait, especially wait in line to buy a product. So if you did a good job of building a large tip, get an assistant who can take money and hand customers the product. That way you can start your pitch again as new people wander by, which gives you the added benefit of new people seeing others buy the product and wonder what the excitement is about. (Plus, remember people hate to go first, so if you can start your pitch again while customers are buying, then the new people are more likely to buy, too.)

It is *much* harder to build a tip from scratch than it is to keep one going. The same holds true in business. Use the fact that you landed one client to help land another. For example, just before you finish a project for one company, call a similar company and say, "We just created a beautiful sales brochure and social media marketing campaign for XYZ Company—do you have any product lines that could use a similar boost in sales?"

The lesson: Once you find you are losing money because you are spending time on administrative work when you could be generating sales, it's time to hire a helper to keep the money flowing. Keep doing what you do best (pitching, writing, etc.) and let your assistant handle the billing and collection.

7. Be open to new opportunities.

Never in my wildest dreams did I ever think I'd be selling Ginsu knives to make money. Me, a graduate of Tulane University with a degree in Computer Engineering! But you know what? I can't even begin to estimate how much that year I spent selling Ginsu knives has furthered my career.

After that summer, interviewing was a breeze. I used to be nervous when interviewing, but no longer. If I can stand on a soap box and sell Ginsu knives to a crowd of fifty sales-resistant show attendees, I can certainly sell my services in a one-on-one interview!

I learned how to attract positive attention, be interesting, be *heard*.

I learned how to pitch ideas, to state my case, to sell my point of view.

I learned how to communicate the benefits of what I was selling, and I learned to ask for the sale.

When was the last time you learned a new skill? Spoke at a conference? Asked for a raise?

Be bold. Take a fork in the road you might not normally choose. You never know where it might lead!

A Turning Point

At the end of the six-month contract I took after selling Ginsu knives, the company for whom I was working wanted to convert me from a contract to perm (staff) writer.

Knowing I was about to enter a negotiation for my salary, I did my homework and gathered metrics I could use to justify the compensation I wanted. (More on workplace negotiation later in the book.)

The company had published metrics for estimating documentation projects (so many pages per day or hours per page). I added up all the work I produced in the six months I was there and discovered I had been twice as productive as the published metric.

So when they asked me what my salary expectations were, I said I wanted twice as much as what they paid the average writer there—a reasonable request, I thought, since I was twice as productive as the average writer.

"Oh no," they replied, "this is how much writers make here. No deviations."

In the split second that followed, I realized I would never be an employee again.

I just wasn't willing to accept that my standard of living would be dictated by an arbitrary number in an arbitrary spreadsheet, as opposed to being compensated based on my *production*.

So I turned down the job offer and started my own business.

I'm not saying you would have made the same decision I did, as there are those who are far more risk adverse than I.

For example, a friend was going through a messy divorce, and it was more important for her to have a steady, predictable income and benefits for her children than it was to have the freedom (and risk) of being a business owner.

My intention is not to tell you which path to take in life, but to remind you that when you are faced with such a decision, do your homework, weigh your own importances, then take the fork in the road that is best for you at that time. You can always change your mind later.

That was a major turning point in my career.

Keep an eye out for yours.

Stop. Breathe. Think. Then Act.

For years I wanted to learn to scuba dive, but didn't have the time or money to do so. But eventually as I paid off more and more debt and saved enough money to spend some on entertainment, I finally decided to take a class.

After passing the book-learning part of the class, my instructor lead me through a series of drills that teaches you how to properly set up your gear—and what to do if something goes wrong. For example, you learn how to clear your mask when it fills with water, how to free your tank if you get caught on something, etc.

And while the lessons went well, I cannot say I was totally confident in my abilities. (This feeling was compounded by the instructor flippantly brushing aside my concerns saying, "You'll do fine. You'll do fine.")

The next step was to get an open-water checkout, where you do all the tasks you drilled—but in open ocean in forty feet of water. Even though the instructor said I was doing fine, I didn't feel like I was. In the end, I decided to postpone the open-water checkout and complete it at a later date. (And with another instructor.)

Eventually, I found an instructor who could do my final checkout—and I couldn't have been happier: My new instructor was as patient and attentive as my last was impatient and superficial. Anytime I did a drill where I didn't feel 100% confident in my abilities, she'd say, "Do it again!"

And I did, again and again, until I *knew* I had the specific skill we were practicing down cold.

My new instructor did another thing my first instructor hadn't. She stated over and over: "Any time anything goes wrong (and things will go wrong): Stop. Breathe. Think. Then act."

She explained that the only time divers get into trouble is when they panic. They make fear-based decisions, they forget to breathe, and they forget their training. Even if your tank is out of air and you are in forty feet of water, you still have enough time for a controlled assent—and you'll even get another sip of air as the gas in your tank expands as you get closer to the surface.

But you won't get that sip if you panic and spit the regulator out of your mouth.

So you have to Stop. Breathe. *Think.*

As fate would have it, I had to follow that advice on my very next dive. After receiving my certification, I went diving with a local tour company. I was traveling alone, so they assigned me a "buddy" on the boat. When diving, you and your buddy are supposed to check each other's equipment before you dive, and then stick together once in the water. This guy did neither. But I was so new to diving, I didn't think to insist he did.

Then I made another mistake: As a newly certified diver, I was trained to dive to sixty feet (eighteen meters). But on the day we went diving, the water was too choppy for a reef dive, so the divemaster took us to a sunken ship one hundred feet down—outside my training limit.

As you dive deeper, the air bubbles in your wetsuit contract. This makes you less buoyant, so you compensate by adding air to your buoyancy compensation device (BCD), a device similar to a life vest that you inflate or deflate as needed to stay neutrally buoyant at any particular depth.

We began the dive and I started descending towards the wreck. I began to sink faster as the bubbles in my wetsuit contracted, so I reached for the hose to put more air in my BCD to compensate.

The hose wasn't there.

I was descending too fast, couldn't find the hose, couldn't control my sinking, and was approaching the bottom (100 feet!) with no buddy to be seen.

And as if things couldn't get worse, I hit the current coming around the end of the ship and start drifting away from the wreck, away from my (missing) buddy, and away from the group.

I started to panic.

But then those words my instructor said over and over popped into my head: "Stop! Breathe! Think!"

Stop: I stopped, literally overriding the primeval urge to shoot back to the surface (and possibly rupturing a lung in the process).

Breathe: I noticed that rather than holding my breath, I was doing the opposite: hyperventilating. So I forced myself to relax, to take long, slow breaths (which helped to calm my panic and clear my head).

Think: I assessed the situation: I wasn't wildly venting air as would be the case if the hose had been cut, so I knew it had to be there *somewhere*. And since I had practiced what to do when gear gets fouled, I took off my BCD, un-fouled the hose (it was caught under the shoulder strap), and put everything back on.

Crisis averted.

All because I remembered to Stop. Breathe. Think. Then act.

And because I practiced, practiced, *practiced* my pool drills until I was certain I knew what I was doing.

So why this long story about scuba diving in a book about career advice? Because I can't tell you how often I apply "Stop. Breathe. Think." in the work-a-day world.

Want to send an angry reply to an email from your boss? Stop! Breathe! Think!

Are you participating in a negotiation (perhaps for a job offer) and it's not going your way? Take a break and rethink your strategy.

Is something going wrong at work and everyone is looking to you to fix it? Don't panic or start the blame game. Stop. Breathe. *Think*.

A problem is only a problem because you don't know what to do about it. I prefer to not even call such situations "problems" because problems have no solution (otherwise they wouldn't be problems, right?). Instead, I label such events "unaddressed situations." Because no matter how bad things look when you are one hundred feet down and can't find your air hose, all you need to do is stay calm, assess the situation, and find a solution.

Do you have a situation in your job, your career, your life, that seems unsolvable?

Stop. Breathe. Think. Then act.

There *is* a solution. You just need to find it!

Overcoming Inertia

Inertia Noun A body at rest tends to stay at rest. A body in motion tends to stay in motion.

I awoke one day at o-dark-hundred to an achingly cold, rainy morning. I hit the snooze button, curled back under my perfectly warm down comforter, and listened to the sound of the rain on my bedroom windows.

"I really should get up," I kept thinking. Today was a gym day and that cheesecake I had last night with dinner wasn't going work itself off. "But I don't want to," said the voice in my head that likes sleeping in on cold, rainy mornings.

After a few more self-indulgent minutes, the voice in my head changed from Sleepy Jack to the Carrie-Anne Moss character in *The Matrix* saying, "Get up, Trinity. Get…UP!"

Well, ok, fine. I got up, made some coffee, and headed to the gym.

When I got to the gym I discovered that despite the steady cold drizzle, the pool was open (I was in Northern Florida for the holidays, so the pool was outside).

And there, posted on each side of the pool, were two lifeguards on duty—alert but hunched with rain gear over their shoulders in a gallant effort to stave off the achingly cold rain.

That put my effort to overcome morning inertia in perspective. I just had to show up, do some laps, and leave. The lifeguards, on the other hand, had to wake up even earlier than I did, open the pool, then sit there under the rain for hours—all so I could show up for some convenient exercise.

At the end of my workout I felt great and was energized to seize the day, but I had come very close to not going at all and sleeping half the day away.

On the drive home I started looking at other tasks I tend to put off. Folding laundry. Filing my taxes. Cold calling to find jobs to fill.

And the funny thing is, once I start such tasks I normally dispatch them fairly quickly. My challenge is not doing, but starting.

What have you been putting off because the voice in your head says, "I don't want to"?

The trick to overcoming inertia is simply starting.

A body in motion tends to stay in motion.

The rest will take care of itself!

Bonus Points:

If you remember your high school physics, *Momentum = Mass x Velocity*. So if you have one of those days when you really don't want to start but do it anyway, just think of all the momentum you'll have to power through your To Do list and brush aside challenges throughout the day!

Food for thought.

Overcoming Fear

I love scuba diving, skydiving, flying powered hang gliders, etc.

It's not that I love adrenaline; it's that I love *freedom*.

Both scuba diving and flying offer something you just can't get on land: the ability to float, to soar, to move in any direction at will.

Jacques Cousteau describes this beautifully:

> *"From birth, man carries the weight of gravity on his shoulders. He is bolted to earth. But man has only to sink beneath the surface and he is free.*
>
> *"Buoyed by water, he can fly in any direction—up, down, sideways—by merely flipping his hand. Under water, man becomes an archangel."*

By now you know that I love to fly, dive, and jump out of airplanes. But what you don't know is… I also have a fear of heights.

Many moons ago, a friend asked me to go to Las Vegas with him to ride the amusement rides for his birthday. One of the rides was at the top of the Stratosphere Hotel, where they hang you over the edge of the building (1,148 feet above ground!) in a little car contraption. And of course, my friend wanted to be in the front row. Oi! You should have seen me inching my way along the line, waiting for our turn.

Was I scared? Absolutely.

Did do it anyway? You betcha.

And I had a blast!

I had several life-changing realizations that day:

The fear I experienced anticipating the ride was far greater than what I experienced during the ride itself.

Once I got past the fear, the ride was pretty fun.

Fear is just an emotion, like anger or enthusiasm. I wouldn't let enthusiasm stop me from doing something, why should I let fear stop me?

I realized I don't have a fear of heights, I have a fear of *falling*. There's a difference.

I get the heebie-jeebies looking over the edge of a third-floor balcony, but can bank a powered hang glider at 2,000 feet without blinking. The difference is that when I'm flying I know that I'm safely buckled in my harness, I'm in firm control of what I'm doing, and that the plane has a 1:8 glide ratio so even if something does happen to the engine, I can still safely land.

Ditto for scuba diving. I've been in situations that were a tad scary, but I learned how to dive safely, drilled what to do in emergencies, and (more importantly) learned how prevent them in the first place.

Fear isn't some nebulous thing that just hangs around like the smell of burnt popcorn cooked too long in a microwave. There is something *about which* one is fearful: The fear of falling, the fear of public speaking, the fear of losing one's job, the fear of running out of air.

So one learns to wear a safety harness when climbing, to have multiple sources of income and money set aside for emergencies, to know your material *cold* before going on stage, to monitor your air consumption and always dive with a buddy.

The key to overcoming fear is training and practice (which leads to competency).

And, of course, not letting fear stop you but carrying on anyway.

You are greater than your fears. They are not greater than you.

Is there something you've always wanted to do?

Take a class.

Do your drills.

Learn to *fly*.

Keep Swimming

There was another time I woke up feeling blah and not wanting to go to the gym and swim laps, but again decided to get up and go (overcome inertia), knowing I'd be fine once I got there.

I arrived, but still wasn't into doing cardio. Finally I decided to make it a game instead of a chore, and consider each end of the lane a "goal" that I could make.

When I accomplished one goal, I turned around and started on the next one.

When I got physically tired of freestyle swimming, I got a kickboard and worked just my legs. When my legs got tired, I switched to those floaty things you put between your feet and I swam with just my arms.

Many laps into this I got winded, so I paused to catch my breath, then continued on.

That's when I had a few realizations:

In life I sometimes wonder if I will make some of my goals or if they are even possible, and consider giving up. When I was swimming, I never considered that the end of the pool (my goal) wasn't there or wasn't attainable. I knew it was there, I just had to keep swimming until I got there. Even when I got winded I just stopped, caught my breath, and continued on. Eventually I got there.

At one point, what I was doing to reach my goal wasn't working any longer (freestyle swimming) so I switched to a kickboard. When that stopped working I switch to a floaty. Each time something changed or presented an obstacle, I just changed tactics and pressed on. Eventually I got there.

In that pool, eighty-eight laps equals a mile. I'm sure at one point I'll work up to being able to do eighty-eight laps non-stop, but that was too big a target to attempt when I first started. I knew, however, I could do one length of the pool, so that was my first goal. I achieved that goal and set another. Made that one and set another. And another. And finally that added up to "Cardio Done."

What goals do you want to reach today? This month? This year?

Write them down with a deadline for each.

Make the first one, then the next, then the next. Pretty soon you'll be swimming a mile non-stop too!

Section 2: DO IT
How to Get a New, Better Job

This section of the book addresses the mechanics of landing jobs and advancing your career.

It dispels the myths about resumes that "everyone knows" are true (but aren't), increases your chances of getting an interview, provides tools you can use to ace interviews once you *get* them, and shows how to find work in a recession.

Need a job? Want a better job?

Keep reading!

What Is a Resume?

According to *Cambridge Dictionary*, "A resume is a written statement of your education and work experience, used especially when you are trying to get a new job."

Wiktionary.com says, "A resume is an account of one's employment history and qualifications often for presentation to a potential future employer when applying for a job."

Both of these definitions are wrong.

So if your resume is not a summary of what you have done, and not a summary of what you can do, then what is a resume?

> *A resume is a vehicle that shows whether or not you match what the reader is looking for.*

And that's all it is.

A resume is not your life story. It's not a capabilities overview. It's just a vehicle that (hopefully) shows that you have what the reader is looking for.

This may be a controversial definition, but is it a good definition? Well, how can you tell if a definition is good?

If you get more interviews as a result of using it, it's a good definition. Keep it. If you get fewer interviews as a result of using it, it's not a good definition. Discard or change it.

Never blindly follow anyone's advice (even mine) without verifying for yourself that it works. In fact, you could rephrase this to cover any advice you ever get from anyone about anything:

If it works for you, it's true, keep it. If it doesn't work for you, it's not true, discard or change it.

As a recruiter, the most common question I'm asked is how long a resume should be. Some "experts" say two pages, some say one, some no more than five. How can someone who doesn't know you or how much experience you have give some arbitrary number and tell you that's *the* number?

Let's circle back to my definition of a resume.

Assuming a resume is just a vehicle that shows that you match what the reader is looking for, how long should your resume be?

Long enough to show you match what the reader is looking for!

If you can do that in a page, do it in a page! If it takes five pages, take five pages.

Consider this: There are only two situations in which someone would read your resume.

- You sent it to them, solicited or unsolicited.
- They found it somewhere (in a resume database, on a job board, etc.)

You may have sent your resume to someone in response to a job posting. You may have sent it to a company in the hopes of working there with no particular job in mind. You may have posted it on every website under the sun, moon, and stars, hoping that someday somebody somewhere would find you and give you a job.

But why you sent your resume doesn't matter. What does matter? Why someone is *reading* it.

And why would someone read your resume? To see if you have what he or she is looking for!

So my definition works for this too.

What readers are looking for may be industry experience, tools and technology, domain knowledge, or something else entirely. You may not know exactly what they're looking for, but you do know one thing—they're looking for *something*.

And if you know that they are looking for something, you can take proactive steps to help them find it.

All right, let's take this a step further. What's wrong with the following definition?

> *A resume is a short account of one's career and qualifications, prepared typically by an applicant for a position.*

It doesn't take into account that the reader is looking for something, and judging whether or not you have it.

So let's combine my definition with that definition, and you get:

> *A resume is short account of one's career and qualifications, typically prepared by an applicant for a position that shows how the applicant matches what the reader is looking for.*

That's a workable definition!

If you know a resume is a vehicle that shows how you match what the reader is looking for, you can take proactive steps to help the reader find what he or she is looking for, and thus increase the number of interviews you will receive.

What Are Managers Looking For?

When reviewing resumes, managers or recruiters are asking themselves seven questions about you:

1. **What are you?**

   Are you a computer programmer? A ditch digger? A chef?

2. **Do you have experience in my industry?**

   Network companies usually want people with network experience, medical companies want medical experience, etc.

3. **How senior are you?**

   Are you entry level? Do you have two years of experience? Five? Ten?

4. **Do you have experience with the tools we use?**

   Every industry has specific tools they use—programming languages, authoring tools, sales-tracking tools. Be sure to show you have what the employer needs.

5. **Do you have a degree?**

   Is it in a related field? Do you have industry-specific certifications?

6. **Are you local?**

   Some people don't want to include their home address in their resumes (darn those witness protection programs!). If you don't want to include your address, at least include your city and state so the reader can see if you are local.

7. Can I afford you?

Are you making $20,000 a year? $50,000? $500,000? (This is the only question not answered in your resume.)

When sending your resume for a job opening, be sure to tailor it to show you have exactly what they are looking for (the job requirements).

What if You Are Not an Exact Match?

Few things are as annoying to a recruiter or hiring manager as wading through stacks and stacks of resumes from candidates who are just not qualified for the job.

However, there's no reason you can't query the person before applying. "Dear Hiring Manager, the job requires ten years of experience with a bachelor's degree in biology; I only have five years of experience but I have a PhD in microbiology and organic chemistry. Would you still consider my resume?"

They may say, "Sure send it over," or "No, we really want somebody with ten." But that way, you didn't waste their time sending a resume for a job that you're not qualified for, it shows you have communication skills, that you read the requirements, and that you're honest.

Dirty Little Resume Secrets

Here are a few little-known facts about the job hunting process. If you know what really happens when a company reads your resume, you can take action and increase your chances of getting interviews.

1. **No one will ever read your resume.**

   People may scan it, read parts of it, search for keywords in it, but no one's going to read your resume from beginning to end and weep at the sheer beauty and brilliance of your writing, your creative spelling, and your mastery of the English language. We just don't have the time.

2. **You will never be hired because of your resume.**

   You'll be rejected because of your resume, weeded out because of your resume, even mocked and scorned because of your resume (and believe me, we mock and scorn).

   So if you do get an interview, it won't be because someone liked your resume—*it will be because you weren't rejected yet.*

   If you've never been a hiring manager, here's how companies decide who to interview: They take a stack of resumes (printed or online) and divide them into two categories: *Maybe* and *No.*

   The reviewer will scan the resumes and think to him/herself, "No…no…maybe. No…maybe…no…no. OK, let's bring in these two for an interview."

   No hiring manager has ever said, "OMG, look at this resume! We must hire this person *immediately*!"

It just doesn't work like that.

Even if you are an exact match, most companies have been burned by candidates who say they have the experience needed but really don't. So even if you look like a great match on paper, in the company's eyes you're still a "maybe."

So if do you get called in for an interview, it won't be because they loved your resume, *it's because you weren't rejected yet.*

Which brings us to:

The longer your resume, the greater the chance you'll be rejected.

I've rejected many candidates who had twelve-plus page resumes because I just wasn't finding what I was looking for. However, not once have I ever rejected a candidate because his or her resume was too short.

There have been times where a resume shows the person has the experience required, but is short on details. When that happens, I'll call or email and ask for more information.

But notice what happened: He/she got me to pick up the phone and call, which is really a phone interview if you think about it.

If you're going to err in your resume, err on the side of brevity, and save the details for the interview.

Companies will use your resume to reject you, so give them as little ammunition as possible.

3. You are writing for a Short Attention Span Theater.

This takes "no one will read your resume" to a whole new level. Not only will people not read your entire resume, they probably won't even read entire *paragraphs*. We're talking short attention spans. Short!

This is another reason I say a resume should be long enough to show that you match what the reader is looking for, *and no longer*.

4. Tailor your resume to show you match the job requirements.

Most job applicants suffer from what I call "misevaluation of importances."

You should evaluate what is important to the reader, and highlight that information in your resume. For example, if you're applying for an engineering writing job and your degree is in computer engineering, put that at the top of your resume. If you majored in English, you may want to put that at the bottom.

While you may think that having an English degree makes you more qualified for a writing job, consider your audience. If an engineer is evaluating your resume, he/she may think someone with "just" an English degree couldn't possibly understand software engineering well enough to document it.

Evaluate what is important to the *reader*, and show that information in your resume early and often.

Here's a real-life example: A company once called me looking for a contract technical writer with patent-writing experience. I found someone and submitted him, and the manager emailed me back ten minutes later saying, "He doesn't have patent-writing experience."

He did have patent-writing experience, but it didn't appear in his resume until the middle of a bulleted list in the middle of the second page. The manager just didn't read that far. (Remember, short attention spans!)

What made matters worse is the resume had a summary that said, "Ten years of experience writing user manuals, policies and procedures…"

What it should have said is, "Ten years of experience writing patent applications, user manuals, policies and procedures..."

Had the hiring manager read that as the first line of the resume she would have thought, "That's exactly what I'm looking for!" and would have continued reading to see where he did it. Instead, she rejected him as not being qualified.

Show you match what the reader is looking for at the very top of your resume, or people will stop reading and reject you as unqualified.

5. **Employers automatically assume you are not qualified for the job for which you are applying.**

Why? Because 95–99% of the resumes they receive are not qualified for the job for which they are sent, so they just assume you're one of the 95% until you prove otherwise. This is another reason your resume must show at the very top that you have what the reader is looking for. Otherwise, we stop reading because it confirms our assumption that you aren't qualified.

And yes, that absolutely means that you have to tailor your resume for each job you apply for. I hate to tell you that, but it's true.

To maximize your chances of getting an interview, tailor each resume you submit to show how you match the job requirements.

The T-Bomb

The smallest typo or formatting error can scuttle your chances of getting an interview.

One. That's all it takes.

One.

I used to say engineers could get away with typos in their resumes, but writers and other content professionals cannot. I don't believe even that is true anymore.

A manager once commented about a software engineer who had typos in her resume. "If she can't write two pages of error-free resume, how can I possibly expect her to write 10,000 lines of error-free code?"

Most people are so familiar with what they think is in their resume that they can't effectively proofread their own work.

Take my advice and have someone else proofread your resume, preferably a professional proofreader. If you don't have access to a real pro, give it to ten people to review. Each person might find a different typo, with no one finding them all.

Current Experience

Whatever companies are looking for, they want you to be doing it in your current job (or your last job if you're not currently working).

For example, if a company has a process engineering project, they'll want someone who is currently doing process engineering. There's an illogical assumption that somebody who's doing it now is better than someone who's not currently doing it, no matter how many years of experience the other person may have. This is why it's so hard to break into a new field: companies are looking for someone who is currently doing the job, not someone who has done it, or can do it.

I'll give you an example, a real-life story. I have a client that manufactures "thin film deposition" machinery. Circuits need to be so thin now that the only way to make them is to take a piece of gold, hit it with a laser until it vaporizes and the gold vapor falls down (deposits) onto the silicon, then etch the really thin gold deposition into a circuit.

A hiring manager at this company wanted a technical writer with current experience in FrameMaker (an authoring tool used for creating large manuals) to document a new machine they were making. I found somebody who had experience documenting thin film deposition technology, but his FrameMaker experience was over six months old.

I knew the manager wasn't going to like this, so I grilled this person about his FrameMaker experience. I had him send me samples. I asked him every FrameMaker question I knew. He did brilliantly—the guy knew his stuff.

Plus he had thin film deposition experience. What was the chance of that?

So I submitted him, and the hiring manager immediately replied, "I told you I wanted someone with *current* FrameMaker experience!"

I'm thinking, "Why? FrameMaker hasn't changed in the past six months." I asked the manager to at least talk with him, look at his samples, perhaps give him a FrameMaker test.

But no joy. The hiring manager had a fixed idea that the experience had to be current. At that point, I realized I was not working with a sane person and stopped working with that manager.

The point of this story? Even if you have done what a company is looking for, you may not get an interview if you're not *currently* doing it. Sorry, but it's true. (Don't shoot the messenger.)

So what can you do to get around that? Figuratively speaking, you slap them in the face with what they're looking for, right at the top of your resume. Then go into details about your previous jobs in direct ratio that the experience matches the current requirements.

In other words, I don't want to see two-and-a-half pages of your current job before I get to the previous one that has the experience I'm looking for.

If you are a full-time staff employee applying for a full-time staff position, I suggest you use a hybrid format: a summary of your skills that shows how you match the job requirements followed by a standard chronological resume. Remember to put minimal details about your current job and much more detail about the job that shows your applicable experience.

If you're a contractor, put something like, "1989 to present, independent contractor working on projects such as…" and list your contracts in the order that they relate to the job to which you're applying. It is much less important for a manager to know the exact dates of your contract than to see right up front that you match the job requirement.

For more information and tips on how to format your resume, read *Get the Job: Optimize Your Resume for the Online Job Search* by Pamela Paterson.

What You Do Is More Important than What You're Called

What you do in your job is more important than your actual job title.

It's been a few pages since we discussed what a resume is, so let's revisit that:

> *A resume is just a vehicle that shows you match what the client is looking for.*

Whenever you are trying to decide what to put in your resume and what to leave out, run it through this filter:

- If it helps show that you match what the reader is looking for, leave it in.
- If it doesn't, leave it out or change it.

We also established earlier that your resume is not your life's history, showing every detail of every job you've ever had.

Take job titles. "Everyone knows" you should list your exact job title on your resume, right? Perhaps not.

Say you are working as a technical writer but the title on your offer letter was, "Information Engineer," or worse—"Member of Technical Staff."

In such cases, listing your exact job title on the resume works against you, as the company is looking for a technical writer, not an "information engineer."

To better help companies find you, list what you do in your job, not what you are called.

Let's take this concept a step further.

Suppose you perform two main activities in your job. For example, you're a technical writer and a courseware developer, but your title is just "technical writer." If you only list "technical writer" on your resume and apply for a courseware developer position, a short-attention-span manager might just skim your job titles and think, "He's not a courseware developer."

Now if you list what you do (not what you're called), your resume would say "Technical Writer/Courseware Developer." Does that help communicate that you match what the reader is looking for?

Yes! So keep it in.

Note: If you are filling out a job application and it asks you for your title, then by all means list your exact title. But by the time a company is asking for an application, you've probably already received an interview and perhaps have an offer pending.

List what you do in your resume and your actual title in a job application, or list what you do *and* your job title, such as Technical Writer/Information Engineer.

This is also important for people trying to transition into a new career.

Say you are a sales engineer where half the time you did sales support and the other half the time you did technical writing (you wrote proposals, specifications, etc.). If you apply for a technical writing job and your last three job titles say, "Sales Engineer, Sales Engineer, Sales Engineer," you're probably not going to get an interview because they are looking for a Technical Writer.

If you put "Sales Engineer/Technical Writer" and apply for a technical writing job, they'll see you've been doing tech writing for the past twenty-two years.

I know this to be true because that's how I got my first technical writing job!

The Top Ten Mistakes Professionals Make When Looking for Work

These mistakes are presented in the order in which people make them. Some are more serious or fatal than others.

1. Not following submission directions

That old adage that you only get one chance to make a first impression is true. I'll give you an example: There are times when a client calls me in a panic, saying the person they had lined up to do a job cancelled at the last minute, and they need someone to start tomorrow morning.

In such cases, I don't have three days to leisurely call people asking if they are available. Instead, I'll send an email to my list saying something like, "A client has an immediate need for a Project Manager in Dallas with experience in the nuclear regulatory industry. If you are interested and available, send me your resume, a summary of your nuclear regulatory experience, and what your bill rate is because I don't have a published bill rate."

The intent is for me to review the information, forward it to my client, and get the person started ASAP.

What often happens instead is that candidates reply to my email saying, "Here's my resume." (Normally those people aren't qualified; that's why they didn't give me the summary. Qualified candidates are usually quite happy to show they are qualified.)

But if you're applying for a job for which there are thirty applicants (which is not uncommon in these economic times) and 50% of the people followed the submission directions, and 50% didn't, who do you think we're going to consider first?

For more on what to do if it's been awhile since you applied and you haven't heard back, see the chapter "Following Up" on page 69.

2. Not building professional relationships

Get to know people. Work your network. Go to conferences, meetings, Meetups. There are jobs that are never posted on Monster.com or Dice.com, but you'll hear about them through networking.

Also, get to know a recruiter. I like being able to put a face with a name, perhaps view your portfolio ahead of time. Plus, when a great job comes in, who do you think we're going to call first? People we know personally.

3. Showing bad manners

It is poor form to email your resume to forty-five recruiters in one email, especially when you list them all in the "To" field— particularly when I'm recruiter number forty-one!

Keep a log of where your resume has been sent. Notice how I phrased that. I did not say where *you* sent your resume; I said where your resume has been sent. This includes where recruiters have sent your resume.

It's bad manners to allow a recruiter to spend time preparing your resume only to find you've already applied for the job directly.

I understand there are anonymous job postings. Some companies will post a job to, say, Craigslist, and hide the company's name so you don't really know which company it is. But that's different.

4. Applying for jobs for which you're not even remotely qualified

Pay attention to the "must have" versus the "nice to haves." I am not saying don't apply for jobs that are a stretch, but do at least be in the ballpark.

5. Not summarizing how your experience matches the job requirements

Here's the biggie. If you learn nothing else from this book, learn this:

> *The biggest mistake people make when job hunting is not summarizing how their experience matches the job requirements.*

No recruiter has time to read your resume from top to bottom. Don't make the recruiter or HR manager go looking for the information; summarize it.

If your cover letter said:

> *"Dear Recruiter,*
>
> *I'm interested in job EN1234. Here's a summary of how my experience matches the job requirements. I'm available at this number to be contacted for an interview.*
>
> *Sincerely,*
>
> *Me"*

... and you included a table that listed *Job Requirement... My Experience...,* you'd go to the front of the line! All I would have to do as a recruiter is check yes...yes...yes. Great! Off you go to the next person in the hiring process.

6. Having an unprofessional resume and email name

Recruiters receive tens if not hundreds of resumes a day. If your resume gets separated from your email, I am going to have to find it—all the harder if your resume is named resume.doc or resume.pdf.

Name your resume so it can be identified: JoeJones.doc, or MarySmith.pdf, or even TomDallyProjectManager.pdf.

Now about your email address:

I'm going to share with you some actual email addresses people have used to apply for jobs. I changed them around to protect the innocent. If any of you are on this list, I apologize.

A little.

> nomangoforyou@hotmail.com
>
> okokok53@hotmail.com
>
> antlers@mrmoose.org
>
> Monkeyboy10@yahoo.com (which means there's nine other monkey boys out there!)
>
> Addictedtocoffee@aol.com (that was a programmer. I'm not going to say that's a bad quality in a programmer.)
>
> realcranky@yahoo.com
>
> hurrythehellup@yahoo.com

Who would hire somebody whose email address is "real cranky"? I want to put RealCranky and HurrytheHellUp in the same room just to see what would happen.

You are trying to make a good first impression. As in naming your resume, use a professional-sounding email address, such as firstname_lastname@gmail.com.

As an aside, I heard an interesting comment not too long ago that if you have an AOL email address, you are old and not with the program. I took offense to that because I *have* an AOL email address. I may be old, but I'm still with the program!

I've kept my AOL address because I have no desire for Google to monitor my email and try to sell me stuff (GoogleAds, altered search results, etc.). Case in point: a technical writer friend of mine posted on Facebook that he did a Google search for something, and the first hit to come up was tech-comm related. This sounded suspicious to me so I did the same search and got a completely different (but expected) search result. I asked him if he had a gmail account and he said, "Yes, why?"

I replied, "Because Google is using the information in your emails to give you what it *thinks* you want to see. <end of soapboxing>

To reduce spam, create a separate email address (with a professional-sounding name) for your job search that you can delete after you find your new job.

7. Having WIIFM (what's in it for me?) objectives

If you are going to include an objective in your resume, simply put the type of job for you are applying, such as "contract project manager" or "full-time software engineer."

Whatever you do, avoid using WIIFM objectives: "I want a company that will value me as an individual and let me grow my personal and technical skills."

I hate to be the one to break this to you, but companies don't care about what you want the company to do for you—they want to know what *you* can do for *the company*. For example, "Objective: To help companies create content marketing campaigns that increase revenue and market share."

One can also be too specific: "Objective: Work within a fast-paced documentation team to develop structured customer assistance documentation using single sourcing, XML-based content management system tools to deliver customer user guides, system administrator installation guides, programmer APIs, STKs, and Internet-delivered training support."

Where are you going to find a job like that? (I looked to see if the applicant was parroting back the description of the job for which he was applying, but in this case he wasn't.)

8. **Providing too much personal information**

If you are applying for a job in the United States, do not include your photograph. It's against the law in this country to discriminate based on age, sex, and a bunch of other stuff. (You include photos in European countries, but not in the U.S.)

Also, don't list your hobbies. (I really don't care that you're into sewing sock monkeys.)

I hate to bring this up, but age discrimination does exist, so don't give people ammunition with which to reject you. Take the dates off your education, and only cover the past ten, maybe fifteen years in your resume. (Remember, a resume is not your life history.)

Plus, as I covered earlier, whatever companies are looking for, they want you to be doing it in your current (or immediate past) job, so what you did ten, fifteen, or twenty years ago really isn't germane (especially in the technology field).

9. **Not anticipating questions and answering them**

Companies will wonder about oddities in your resume, such as gaps in your work history. If you haven't been working for the past two years, I want to know why. What have you been doing? Sitting at home watching TV and eating Del Monte cling peaches in heavy syrup? Even if you've been looking non-stop for full-time staff work, you could also have been doing something productive, such as slinging a hammer for Habitat for Humanity or being a docent at a museum—*something* that shows you have work ethic.

If you have been out of work for a while, explain why, or you will look like damaged goods that no one wants to buy. For example, "Reentering the workforce after taking time off to be primary caregiver to my aging parents." Or "Looking for a Content Marketing position after going to school full time to earn my MBA in Digital Marketing."

10. Not keeping your skills current

The saddest thing you can do is to lose a potential job because you didn't keep up with your tools (project management tools, blogging tools, etc.)

I have heard many a candidate profess, "I could learn [that tool] in a weekend," and my answer is always, "Yeah? Then why haven't you?"

You might not become an expert in a weekend, but you can learn the tools well enough to list them on your resume.

Can't afford a full license of every tool you need? Many companies allow you to download trial versions of their products. Another option is to buy used software on eBay. (Just make sure you get the original installation CD and manual to make sure it's not pirated.)

Stay on top of your tools!

Resumes: A Summary

- Find out what the hiring manager is looking for (when possible) and include that in your resume.
- Make sure that information is easy to find because your resume is a vehicle that shows that you match what the reader is looking for.
- Be brief but clear; you are writing for Short Attention Span Theater.
- Do not give people ammunition with which to reject you.
- Have perfect formatting, perfect spelling, perfect grammar, and perfect parallel structure.
- State what you did, not what you were called.
- Keep your skills current.
- When applying for jobs, include a summary of how your experience matches each of the job requirements.

Try this for yourself.

The end result should be more interviews.

Cover Your Letter

Most recruiters and hiring managers skip reading cover letters because they are usually generic letters saying how much you want to work for the company, blah, blah, blah.

True story: I met with one of my clients to go over three candidates I submitted. (Each submission had the candidate's resume and a perfect summary of how their experience matched the job requirements.)

At the meeting I discovered the client never even *opened* the cover letter documents, let alone read them.

So what did I learn from that? What can you learn from that?

Make your cover letter the first page of your resume document, so it is the first thing they see. Of course they may just page down past the cover letter to look at the resume, but hopefully once they see it contains that nice matrix of how you match what they are looking for, they'll read it.

Another story: Before Windows Vista was released, it was codenamed "Longhorn." I was helping a client hire a technical writer, and the documentation manager knew that Longhorn was supposed to have an XML-based help engine (a brand-new way of delivering online help).

The manager liked her staff to keep on top of industry trends, so one of the job requirements was "familiarity with Longhorn help." Not *experience* with Longhorn help because it didn't even exist yet, but just familiarity with what was on the horizon.

A guy applied for the job and had everything the manager was looking for, except—when he got to this requirement on the online application, "Familiarity with Longhorn help," his answer was, "Never heard of it."

This struck me as oddly arrogant so I did an Internet search for "What is Longhorn help?" and the very first hit was an article entitled, "What is Longhorn Help?"

The search took .03 seconds to do.

That one answer was like a door into his soul. This person was so lazy/arrogant/choose-your-favorite-adjective that he didn't take .03 seconds to find out what he'd be doing with the next five years of his life. I knew the hiring manager wouldn't like him, so I didn't submit him—despite the fact that he was highly qualified for the job.

Job hunting is a lot like dating—you're on your best behavior for like the first six weeks or so. So if that was his best behavior, I would hate to see what he'd be like after he got hired.

What if you are *mostly* qualified for the job, perhaps lacking just one or two requests in a list of ten requirements?

This is where you say, "I don't have two years of experience with _____, but I do have one year of _____ and ten years of _____, which are very similar to _____."

If you do nothing else, summarize how your skills match the requirements of the job for which you are applying and see how many more interviews you get.

Following Up

What do you do when you've applied to a job posting that said, "To be considered, send your resume to resumes@company.com. No calls," and it's been three weeks and they haven't called?

If they haven't called and you upset them by calling, what are they going to do, not call more? You really don't have much to lose. But how can you respectfully show that you followed the submission directions and yet try to nudge the cycle along?

Even if the job posting said, "No calls please," there's nothing wrong with calling and saying, "Hi, I applied for a job XYZ three weeks ago, and I have not received a confirmation that my application was received. Could you do me a favor and see if my resume is in the system?"

That would be acceptable.

One woman I met drove over to the company after applying for a job and left a thank you note at reception. They found her name and tracked the resume down that may have been sitting there in the black hole somewhere.

She got the job.

If you're unemployed, it's up to you to be a little more proactive. I'm not going to use "aggressive" because that has a very negative connotation, but proactive, yes.

Getting Interviews

The Internet has to be the absolute *best* tool and the absolute *worst* tool in the history of man when it comes to job hunting. It is the best tool because you can search for any job anywhere in the world and have the results in seconds. It is also the worst tool since it takes all human interaction out of the application process, and with it all possibility of you asserting positive control over your job search.

So what's a job hunter to do?

Make It Personal

By all means, search Internet job boards like Dice.com and Monster.com. Make a list of all the jobs for which you'd like to apply.

If the job posting lists an actual person to whom you can send your resume, send him or her your resume per the submission directions. Then follow up in a week or so if you haven't heard back.

But what should you do if the job description doesn't list a real person, just a link to an online application—or worse, a generic email like jobs@BlackholeNeverToBeHeardFromAgain.com?

There is a datum, a natural law about job hunting:

The better the personal relationship you have with the person to whom you are sending your resume, the better your chances of getting an interview.

For example, what would be your chances of getting an interview if your mother's best friend is the hiring manager with a job opening at XYZ Company?

Pretty good I'd bet.

Conversely, what do you think the relative chances would be of getting an interview if you applied for the same job by just sending your resume to jobs@XYZCompany.com?

Not nearly as good.

I've never been keen on waiting in line with the masses—I try to find a more expedient, personal, and favorable solution. For example, say you are at an airport and your connecting flight is cancelled. Don't wait in line for an agent to handle the forty or fifty people in front of you, pick up a phone and call the airline's reservation number—instantly you are next in line!

A similar approach can be taken when job hunting. When a job is posted on a company or Internet job board, the company will receive tens if not hundreds of resumes from applicants. An even worse scenario is when resumes from all job applicants at a company get sent to one email address (e.g. jobs@XYZcompany.com), as now your resume is not just one of many sent for one job, but is also mixed in with resumes for all other jobs at the company, plus people who are just submitting their resumes to be kept on file, *plus* the inevitable spam that arrives at a company's jobs@ email address.

Do you really want your email application to be just one in a sea of emails and spam in a generic jobs email inbox? (All of which, by the way, are probably processed in the order in which they were received, meaning who knows when they will get around to reading and processing your application.)

Which brings me back to my airport line analogy: how can you avoid having to wait in line until someone gets around to processing your job application?

Locate a job using the Internet boards and then apply for the job using a personal relationship.

And since I assume you don't have family members who are hiring managers, you're going to have to build those relationships.

How many ways are there to build personal (professional) relationships? Plenty!

- Use your professional networks. Go to meetings for professional organizations in your industry and ask if anyone works at XYZ Company. If you find someone, ask that person to pass your resume to the hiring manager. Not only will you stand out by getting a personal referral, but the referring person may get a finder's fee to boot.

- Can't find anyone you know personally who works at XYZ Company? Check professional networking sites like LinkedIn and see if there is anyone at the company to whom you are connected (you know someone who, in turn, knows someone at that company).

  Look for someone who has a similar job who might be in the same department (a tech writer if you are applying for a tech writing job, a project manager if you are applying for a PM job, etc.). But don't be afraid to try a random person at the company if you don't have a connection to a direct counterpart.

  Then ask for an introduction or referral to the hiring manager (or to someone in Human Resources if the connection doesn't know the hiring manager).

- There is a third option that lies somewhere between a personal referral to the hiring manager (best) and emailing your resume to jobs@ (worst): emailing your resume to someone in HR.

Over the past year or so I have observed this curiously illogical phenomenon. Rarely do company websites list HR or recruiter contacts at the company, but almost all corporate recruiters have a profile on LinkedIn because they use LinkedIn as a recruiting asset.

So if you can't find someone that you know at XYZ Company through networking, then contact a recruiter there through LinkedIn and ask if you can send your resume directly to him or her.

He might say "Sure!" or he might say "Apply online and I'll watch for it to arrive." Either way you now have someone who will personally handle your application and pass your resume on to the hiring manager.

And while I have emphasized LinkedIn so far, don't forget other professional and social networking sites, such as Plaxo.com, Facebook.com, MySpace.com, Classmates.com, etc.

Find job openings online, but apply for them via a personal referral.

Be Proactive

I'm always amazed when I hear someone whine about how hard it is to find work given "how bad the economy is." When I ask these same people what they are doing to find work, inevitably they answer, "I posted my resume on Monster.com" or, "I emailed my resume to several companies I saw on Dice."

I'm sorry but that's not job hunting, that's job *waiting*.

Applying for jobs online may work when times are great but is woefully inadequate when times are tough.

So what can you do other than emailing your resume to resumes@ BlackHoleNeverToBeHeardFromAgain.com?

Plenty!

I'll give you a few examples, but keep in mind these are just a few out of hundreds if not thousands of ideas you can try:

- Pick the top ten companies in your area for which you'd like to work, call and ask for a manager there and say "I'm writing an article for [pick a local publication, such as a professional organization newsletter]. May I interview you about hiring trends in our industry?"

  Then ask about their plans to hire contract and permanent people over the next six months. Ask, "Would you like to see a copy of the article when it is published?" Then get their contact info.

  Suddenly, you are on a *first name basis* with the very people who would hire you. You still have to write the article, of course, but now you have a reason to follow up and an opportunity to mention that you, yourself, might be interested in the position if they say they are currently hiring will be hiring in the future.

- Make a list of companies that are currently hiring in any aspect of your industry. Say you are a software tester or software technical writer. Make a list of all the companies currently hiring software engineers. If they are hiring engineers now to code software, eventually they will need people to test and document it.

  So be proactive and contact a recruiter *before* the job is posted. Who knows—you might get the job without it ever being posted. (Remember, advertising costs money. Look at all the money they'll save by hiring you as a result of your well-timed resume submission!)

- I know a technical writer in Orange County, California who goes to the exhibit hall of every trade show held at the OC Convention Center. He goes from booth to booth looking at each company's marketing collateral (brochures, data sheets, etc.). If a company has less than perfect collateral, he asks for the head of sales or marketing (who is often in or around the booth), introduces himself, and says, "Boy, your competitors' brochures look much more professional than yours. I can help make these better!" and hands the person his business card.

  I don't think he's ever been out of work in the more than twenty years I've known him.

These are all examples of how to find work, not how to wait for work to find you.

There are thousands of ways to network, to get referrals, to be more visible than an anonymous email in a generic HR email inbox.

Be proactive.

Be *creative*.

Get the interview.

Be Visible

I know a technical writer who for years went to computer programming user group meetings. She would speak to all the programmers there who wrote their own manuals about how outsourcing the work would not only make their manuals better, but would also free up their time to do what they do best (program).

She may not have received a job at each meeting, but she made sure everyone left with her business card. When these programmers finally did need a technical writer, guess who they called!

That user group is all but extinct now, but to this day (years later) she still gets calls from people who saw her at those meetings and kept her business card on file until they finally needed her services.

I too have networked at meetings, volunteered at events, spoken at conferences. I (as a recruiter) make myself visible to people who might have jobs to fill. I know there is work out there, I just have to find it.

And I do.

By the way, for the introverts who are thinking, "Well that might work for someone as extroverted as Jack, but I could never be a power networker or public speaker!" Well I hate to break your "poor me" bubble, but none of us who do public speaking were born comfortable speaking in public. We learned, we *practiced*. We may have had a fear of public speaking, but gosh darn, we did it anyway.

In hindsight, I can say without a doubt that all the public speaking I've done has helped me find work. Not only did meeting so many people help in terms of finding job leads, but the self-confidence it built was invaluable. (Once you become comfortable speaking in front of 100–200 people, doing a one-on-one interview is a piece of cake.)

A non-profit organization called Toastmasters International helps people learn to be excellent public speakers. Their mission is to "empower individuals to become more effective communicators and leaders."

Sound like something you could use? The organization has over 200,000 members in 11,500 clubs in 92 countries. See their website for a chapter near you: www.toastmasters.org.

Get started. *Now.*

You never know—you just might meet someone with a job opening!

Social Networking

Early web pages were static, meaning all the reader could do was read them. Web 2.0 gave the reader the ability to interact, first giving people the ability to comment on what was published, then eventually to upload content of their own.

People like to ask co-workers or friends about local restaurants, movies, etc., but such recommendations used to be limited by the number of friends and co-workers they had. Web 2.0 changed that, enabling people to get recommendations from anyone anywhere in the world. For example, say you are considering staying at the Sweet Olive Bed and Breakfast in New Orleans. Simply go to TripAdvisor.com and see what people who have stayed there say about that property. From Istanbul to Indianapolis, this is word-of-mouth on a global scale!

Scott Abel (TheContentWrangler.com) describes Web 2.0 this way:

> *"Communication used to be restricted to geography—you would see something on the bulletin board of your local coffee house, and mention it to friend next door or in the next cubical at work. Social networks remove the geographic restriction. Now I share information with friends and acquaintances across the street and across the globe. Facebook is one big world-wide coffee shop!"*

WIIFM?

When Scott Abel shared his world-wide coffee shop analogy with me, he used this example: a contact of his posted a lament one day, "I wish I could get a job in Palm Springs…." A few days later a different contact mentioned they had an opening in Palm Springs, so he introduced them.

I don't have statistics to back this up, but I wouldn't doubt that more job openings are filled through personal referrals than by posting the job to online job sites. In fact, I believe that many positions are filled by employee referrals long before they need to be advertised, and thus are never even posted online.

How many job opportunities are you missing because you are not networking with your industry peers?

A Two-Edged Sword

The up side to the Internet is the easy way people can find information. The down side is that anything you say (or is said about you) is recorded on the Internet forever.

I once saw a bumper sticker that said, "Never do anything you wouldn't want to explain to the paramedics." A similar rule of thumb would be, "Never post anything on the Internet you wouldn't want your employer or grandmother to see."

Companies will often search for you online before they offer you a job, so be careful what you post online.

For example, a friend of mine who I knew to be actively interviewing posted on Twitter that she was sick and going home to open a bottle of wine. While her intent was just to share with her "peeps" what she was doing that evening, a potential employer could look at those same words and think, "Hmm, she is sickly and uses alcohol to cope with stress. Let's go with the other candidate we liked." (I advised her to delete that tweet, which she did.)

Here's a more egregious example. Someone who was offered a job posted the following online: "Big Corp just offered me a job! Now I have to weigh the utility of a fatty paycheck against the daily commute to San Jose and hating the work." Someone from Big Corp saw the post and promptly withdrew the job offer.

The lesson: have an online branding strategy and think twice before posting critical or personal information about yourself on the Internet!

Four Critical Steps to Getting a Job Offer

Most people do not go on interviews prepared with an interviewing strategy—they just answer the questions the interviewer asks, show a few samples of their work, then leave, hoping they did well enough to get a second interview.

Or worse, they let interviewers casually flip through their portfolio, totally missing an opportunity to show the interviewer exactly why they are a good fit for the job, and how they can help the company with their specific business needs.

Have you ever interviewed for a job that you thought went well but didn't result in an offer? If so, chances are you lacked an interview strategy that accomplishes four critical objectives:

1. Understand the job requirements.

2. Establish that you are an expert at what you do.

3. Establish that you really have done what you claim. (That is, show that you have achieved practical results, not just absorbed theoretical knowledge.)

4. Show how you can solve the problems they are experiencing.

By achieving each one of these objectives *in order*, you show a potential interviewer who you are, what you've done, and why you are the best candidate for the job.

1. **Understand the job requirements.**

   Understanding the job requirements is critical to acing any interview because more often than not the requirements in the published job description are not even close to what the hiring manager is really looking for. And asking what each interviewer is looking for also gives you some insight into what the interviewer thinks is important so you can show how you match those exact requirements.

   This is especially true in a large organization where you interview with multiple people before being offered the job. Each person with whom you interview has different priorities. Unless you ask each person what he or she is looking for, you won't know how to show you are a good match.

   Ask each interviewer about the job and how the position fits in the overall product development process. Every company produces *something*. It's up to you to find out how you can help the company make money or save money. If you can do neither, why would they hire you?

   If you know the position has been open for a while, also ask what they have not been finding in other candidates interviewed and then make sure to address those points.

   By *really* understanding exactly what is needed and wanted, you can position yourself as the perfect match as you move the interview forward.

2. **Establish that you are an expert.**

   The next objective in the interview process is to establish you are an expert in your field.

   When I say "expert" I don't necessarily mean someone who has twenty years of experience. To me an expert is some who understands *and can competently apply* the theory of his job *to the level that he has been trained.*

For example, I wouldn't expect an entry-level programmer to be an expert in software design and project management, but I would expect him or her to take a design a more senior person created and expertly code it.

So how do you establish that you are an expert in your field? Show a sample plan you have created and executed.

Software engineers design before they code. Carpenters get a blueprint before they build. Even an executive assistant should be competent in planning organizational projects and then carrying out those plans.

Most companies are not looking for warm bodies just to fill a chair. They are looking for competent professionals who can assess a situation, plan a solution, and execute that plan.

Contrary to popular belief, you are not selling "you" in an interview—you are selling *your ability to get things done.*

What you bring to a potential employer is not your time, but your knowledge, experience, and competence.

In the interview, explain how you go about doing your job. Better yet, have a copy of a plan you have written and executed in your portfolio. Explain each item in the plan, why the information is needed, and why *not* having that information can affect the outcome of the project.

I am a firm believer that an "expert" is someone who has made all the mistakes possible in a given field—assuming you don't keep repeating them.

Use this to your advantage in an interview. After you discuss a project that went well, discuss a project that didn't go according to plan, what you learned from it, and how you revised your "process" to keep that from happening again. If companies see you have learned from past mistakes, they don't have to worry about you making the same mistake there.

And it shows that you can learn, adapt to new circumstances, and rise to new challenges.

Watch interviewers nod their heads in agreement as you walk them through your plan, as you point out aspects they have already considered. And then watch them take interest when you explain aspects of a project they haven't considered!

By the time you finish explaining all the aspects of a plan you've created and executed, the interviewer *knows* you know what you're talking about.

Thus, you achieve the second critical interview objective: the interviewer recognizes you are an expert in your field. (To the level to which you've been trained, of course.)

3. **Establish that you really have done what you claim.**

Once you have explained the importance of a plan you created then executed, show what resulted from the plan to illustrate its success.

If you designed software, show the software you created. If you are an inventor, show the item you invented. If you are an executive assistant who organized a company's annual blood drive, show the thank-you letter from the blood bank, perhaps one that says how many lives were improved as a result of your efforts.

By *showing* what you have built or created, you have achieved the third critical interview objective: establish that you really have done what you claim.

4. Show how you can solve the problems they are experiencing.

By now in the interview you have established that you are an expert in your field and really have done what you claim. But how do you reach the ultimate goal of getting the job offer?

By using a before-and-after sample that shows no matter how bad a problem or need the interviewer has, you can help— because you've already done that for someone else.

In my portfolio I have a really messy engineering drawing that looks like it was scribbled on the back of a napkin. From that really messy drawing, I created a very professional illustration, then dropped the illustration into the document I was writing at the time. All three versions are in my portfolio.

Here is how I use the sample to land the job/contract/project: after I show projects that I have completed, I then say, "Let me show you how the XYZ system was explained to me," and I show my really messy "before" sample.

Almost every time the person laughs, points to a messy diagram or whiteboard in the room, and says, "That is *exactly* how our stuff looks!!!"

Then, *after* the person stops his or her cathartic chuckling, I show the "after" samples—how I brought order to chaos.

At this point, I sit back, *shut up*, and wait for a go button. (In sales talk, a "go button" is anything the other person says that indicates they want to buy.) After the person finally finishes smiling at the before-and-after samples, he/she usually puts them down and says something to the effect of, "OK, how long do you think the project will take?" or "I have one more person to interview but I'd like you to come back so the VP can meet you…" or some other statement expressing the desire to move forward.

You may not have a messy engineering drawing, but I'm sure you have some sort of chaotic source material to use as a "before" sample until you can save a suitably messy drawing from your next project. (And if you're *really* smart, you'll take the person for whom you are working to lunch, hand them the paper napkin and felt tip pen you just *happen* to have with you, and say, "Now show me again what you need/how the system works/how you want the event to look...")

While we may take for granted that it is part of our job to turn chaos into a perfectly humming production machine, the point here is to *show* you can do that. Use before-and-after sales graphs, or perhaps a "before" photograph that shows how messy the company supply room was before you tackled the problem, and an "after" photo of a perfectly organized and spotless room.

By showing radically different before-and-after samples, you achieve the final interview objective: the interviewer decides you can help solve the exact problems the company is having since you've done that for other companies, and thus offers you the job/contract/project.

Summary

A portfolio is an interview tool you can use to control an interview and actively lead an interviewer to the conclusion that that you are *the* person to hire:

1. You took the time to really understand the interviewer's needs.

2. By explaining what goes into a plan you've created, you showed you are an expert in your field.

3. By presenting samples of your work, you showed you really have done what you claim.

4. By showing an incredible before and after sample, you showed you can solve problems such as the ones the interviewer has.

Why would they hire anyone else?

Send Out Ships

You've probably heard the expression, "When my ship comes in."

Any idea where that expression comes from?

In the nineteenth century, merchants in Europe would mortgage everything they owned to build and provision ships to sail to the New World. When (if) the ships finally returned, loaded with furs and spices and other goods, the merchants would be rich beyond their wildest dreams.

However, there wasn't GPS and satellite telephones in those days, so the merchants would go down to the dock each day, literally waiting for their ships to come in.

However, as Chellie Campbell observes in her book, *The Wealthy Spirit*:

> *"Some people are going down to the dock waiting for their ship to come in—but they aren't sending any out!"*

You have to send out ships!

And you can't send out just *one* ship—there are hurricanes and sandbars and mutinies, all of which can prevent your ship from returning. So you have to send out multiple ships.

Every call you make, every business card you hand out, every networking event you attend is a ship that might someday come in.

It may take weeks or years for those ships to come in, but if you send enough out, they *will* come in.

The secret to ongoing prosperity and "job security" is to keep sending out ships.

True story: After starting my own outsource technical writing company, I called the head of documentation at Epson (a leading manufacturer of consumer printers and electronics) and asked if she had any projects to outsource. She said no, her current staff had things covered.

I replied, "Okay, I'll check in again next quarter." And I did. In fact, I checked in every quarter for almost two years. Then, in my next quarterly check-in call, she replied, "Actually, I just got out of a meeting where they gave me a project and I don't have anyone to do it. Come on in!"

That ship coming in was a result of almost *two years* of sending out ships.

And then, after the item I documented hit the market, *PC Magazine* said in a review of the product, "The concise manual made setup easy."

Bingo!

You better believe I put a copy of that review in my portfolio and showed it to every prospective client I met! That one call (two years in the making) has generated ship after ship (new clients)—all because I kept calling and didn't stop after the first "no."

You never know when a ship is going to sail in. In fact, you're not even responsible for getting your ships to sail in. You're just responsible for sending them out.

Gold Calling

While we're on the subject of sending out ships, let's talk about gold calling.

In *The Wealthy Spirit*, Chellie also recommends keeping a log of how many ships you send out each week. (She calls it, simply enough, your Ships Log.)

By recording how many ships and what types of ships you sent (cold calling, going to network lunches, etc.), you can see how many ships out it takes before you get a ship back.

I know from keeping my own logs as a recruiter that it takes me an average of thirty calls and/or emails to customers (or potential customers) before someone says yes, they need my help filling a position.

By *knowing* it takes an average of thirty calls out to get a job in:

- It gives me an idea of how much promotion I have to do before a ship comes in, and
- It takes all the sting out people saying "No" when I ask them for business.

I used to get discouraged when I called someone and they said, "No." Now, because I know I need twenty-nine "nos" before I get a "yes," whenever I get a "no" I think, "YES! Only twenty-eight more nos to go!"

In other words, I know I need twenty-nine nos for a yes, so I look forward to getting them. Each and every no is getting me one step closer to a yes.

And it's not like I'll get an infinity of depressing nos. Because I keep a Ships Log, I know how many nos it takes to get what I want (a new client, a new job to fill, etc.). That makes it a game, not a chore. And I love playing games where I know I'll win if I just play long enough. (In my case, "long enough" is twenty-nine nos.)

Chellie knows this concept so well that she does a daily affirmation, "There's money in the phone and I'm calling me some today!"

She even painted her phone gold and wears gold nail polish on her dialing finger to remind herself. She doesn't even call it "cold calling," she calls it "gold calling"!

There *is* money in the phone. How much do you want?

How many Gold Calls will it take?

Start a Ships Log and find out!

Section 3: HAVE IT
How to Get What
You Really Want in Life

This final section provides tips on how to secure your future and attain your goals (really BIG goals).

It can be done.

You can do it.

Creating the Path

I heard a saying once that went something like, "You don't get to vote on the way things are—you already did." To me this means that the choices you made in the past led you to where you are today, and the choices you make today will determine the opportunities you will have in the future.

I like to take this notion a step further; you not only choose the path you walk, you *create* the path you walk.

Not happy with your current job and/or economic condition? Well, fine—acknowledge the choices you made that led you there, chalk them up to life's lessons, and start creating your tomorrow.

If you look for opportunities (I mean *really* look—don't wait for opportunities to come to you) and develop multiple income streams in multiple industries, you have a better chance of staying employed should one industry "recess" unexpectedly.

If you expand the services you offer, if you build a support team, if you build and maintain your professional networks, you can use each and every one of those channels should you need employment options in the future.

You *create* the career path on which you walk.

Have you decided where you want to go?

Start walking!

Recession-Proof Your Career

I would guess that most of you (if you have gotten this far through the book and are applying what you've been learning) have some form of employment now that pays the bills.

And while you may be itching to jump into a new career as fast as possible, it can take time to build a business or learn a new skill—all of which can come to a screeching halt if you are suddenly laid off in the next recession. (And there will be a next recession sooner or later.)

So before we jump into creating the "perfect" job or career, let's look as some short- and long-term strategies for:

1. Increasing your chances of surviving a layoff.

2. Increasing your ability to find work in case you do get laid off.

One would think that if you do a good job at strategy #1, you wouldn't need strategy #2, but mergers do happen and companies sometimes offshore entire departments, so it's best if you do both to maximize your chances of staying employed.

Increase Your Chances of Surviving a Corporate Layoff

There are three main actions you can take to avoid being laid off:

- Add value to your company.
- Ensure that management recognizes that you add value.
- Repeat as needed.

Add Value to Your Company

The main strategy to staying employed is to make yourself so valuable that your company wouldn't even *consider* letting you go. This isn't as hard to do as you might think.

Here is an excellent example: Andrea Ames is the first person in the history of IBM to rise from an information-development role to her current level in the company.

When people ask her what she does for a living, she replies, "I solve business problems."

Not, "I do business process modeling." Not, "I coordinate changes to the user experience." While she may actually do those things as part of her job, they're not the way she approaches her job, and they are certainly not how she identifies her corporate mission. She finds problems her company is experiencing and then finds solutions.

How does she find problems to solve? She asks for them! Every three months she asks the executives in her division, "What problems are keeping you up at night?" Then she looks at what her group can do to help solve those problems.

Even if the problems are not directly occurring in her area, there are often actions her group can take as part of a larger solution. In short, she strives to be an innovative solution provider and profit center, not a commodity-like cost center.

What a great way to increase your job security! Who in the world would lay off an individual who's continually saving the company money and helping to solve management's problems?

When was the last time you looked for problems to solve in your company or workplace?

Ensure Management Recognizes that You Add Value

I recently started classes at a local business school and was looking forward to applying the information to my career, specifically how to better market my services. However, I soon found out that before I could take the marketing courses I wanted, I had to take a course in public relations (PR).

I was not happy about this since I thought PR was a nefarious undertaking—something done by big corporations to cover up embarrassing events or by politicians wanting to manipulate public opinion. The definition of PR I read in *Public Relations News* certainly supported my viewpoint:

> Public Relations: The management function which evaluates public attitudes, identifies the policies and procedures of an individual or an organization, and executes a program of action to earn public understanding and acceptance.

While that definition might apply to a public relations firm with clients like Exxon or General Motors, I didn't find it very applicable to me.

Next, I read *Effective Public Relations* by Scott Cutlip and Allen Center, who described PR as "empathetic listening and persuasive communication." While this was closer, I knew this definition of PR applied more to defusing a heated labor dispute than advancing my career.

I'm a professional in my field, and the products I create are excellent demonstrations of my ability. But how many people were aware of my good works? Not many.

No one else was taking the time to advertise my accomplishments, so I sat down and wrote a PR plan for myself, working out what I wanted known and who I wanted to promote to.

Suddenly my visibility increased and I started landing new clients. My version of PR worked!

Day in and day out, you are constantly demonstrating that you are a professional in your field.

Do people know?

Get the word out!

Creating a PR Campaign

There are four basic steps to creating a public relations campaign:

1. Research

Don't make the mistake of assuming you know what your audience thinks and feels—find out for sure. Even informal surveys can reveal some surprising results.

2. Planning

Does your company publish a newsletter? Does it post success stories on your intranet? Does it grant awards for accomplishments? Once you have researched ways you can publish your accomplishments, make a plan for what you will do, and create a time line for getting the word out.

3. Communication

If you are a contractor, communicate your accomplishments to prospective clients. If you are an employee, communicate your accomplishments to your current or prospective employers. Make sure people in your company know the value you bring to the organization.

4. Evaluation

As with other endeavors, evaluate your performance at the end of the project. Whether you measure the effectiveness of your PR campaign with a new opinion survey or by an increase in your paycheck, strengthen what worked in your plan and change what didn't. (Then, of course, write and execute your PR plan for the next year and get back to work!)

Be the Captain of Your Career
A New Approach to Career Planning and Advancement

Taking the Initiative

My favorite story about an employee taking the initiative and expanding his sphere of influence is Frank Eliason, a customer service agent from Comcast Cable. Rather than waiting for customers to call him to complain (or worse, simply switching to another carrier without calling), Frank searched for negative comments on Twitter, then proactively reached out to the customers and offered to help.

From Businessweek.com:

> *"I think it's safe to call Comcast's Frank Eliason the most famous customer service manager in the U.S., possibly in the world. Ten months ago, Eliason, whose official title is [now] Director of Digital Care, came up with the idea of using Twitter to interact with customers of Comcast, for whom he has worked for a year and a half."*

Eliason discovered that by doing a search for the word "Comcast" (and occasionally "Comcrap"), he could find tweeters who just happened to mention service complaints he could address.

What customer problem can you solve today?

Blog, Blog, Blog

Since real-time microsites limit the length of each message sent (the Twitter limit is 140 characters), many people include just a few words about a topic and a link to a website for more information.

For example, I recently retweeted an article Chellie Campbell posted about how to set your bill rate:

> **JackMolisani** *Are you happy with your bill rate? Well, who picked that number? RT @ChellieCampbell http://www.chellie.com/newsletter*

The problem with such tweets is that they drive traffic to Chellie's website, not mine. I have to have content on my site to point to if I wanted to use Twitter as a business development tool, so I converted my old "static" website to a blog-based website. Now I am blogging and using Twitter to drive traffic to my site:

> **JackMolisani** *New blog post: How successful do YOU want to be? http://prospringstaffing.com/category/blog/*

You don't have to own your own company or be a consultant to have a blog. Find something interesting that your department or employer is doing and get the word out.

You don't have to be an independent contractor or consultant to take advantage of social networking. You do, however, have to take an active interest in changing business markets and how your company should respond to those changes.

Claiming Your Sphere of Influence

Steve Rosenbaum recently blogged on FastCompany.com about the growing importance of content strategists. Companies are finally getting that customers are not visiting companies' websites for flash, they visit for substance. It's not about the tools, it's about the content, and customers want content germane to them.

"All of us, it now appears, are in the Content business."

I love the part in the Disney film *Finding Nemo* when the seagulls spot food and unabashedly proclaim, "Mine! Mine! MineMineMine!"

We must apply that same passion and assertiveness in carving out and claiming our sphere of influence.

Increase Your Ability to Find Work

Now that we have looked at ways to increase (and promote) the value you bring to your current employer, let's look at some actions you can take in the future to ensure continued employment when the next recession comes along.

There are three main strategies to increase your long-term marketability:

- Expand the industries you serve.
- Expand the services you offer.
- Start your own business.

Expand the Industries You Serve

What can you do if you have been working in, say, accounting companies your entire career and want to move into a new field?

One option is to take classes in different fields—but which fields? What classes will make you the most marketable? That varies depending on the country and region in which you live, so I suggest doing some research.

First, look at what investment advisors are saying are the hot growth industries two, five, and ten years out. If those industries are growing, they will be hiring!

Another option is to monitor the types of jobs being posted on job boards like Dice.com, Monster.com, etc. By monitoring such sites, you can see the types of companies that are hiring in your area, and you can take classes to prepare yourself for those jobs.

Yet another option would be to find someone who already services those industries, preferably an independent contractor or outsource company with projects that can be done off-site. Ask to help with their projects. By gaining experience with just one such project, you can leverage it to get another and another until finally you are well-established in the industries in which you want to expand.

And keep in mind, the more industries in which you can be established, the greater your chances of finding work if any one of those industries slows down.

Expand the Services You Offer

What other services can you offer that companies need and will pay for?

Will it benefit you to go back to school for an additional certificate or degree? Yes. Will that take a few months or a few years? Probably.

But remember, we are talking about how to prepare for the next recession after the economy recovers from its current slump.

And considering it might take a while to get out of *this* slump, you've got plenty of time to prepare for the next one!

Start Your Own Business

One option for taking control of your income and increasing your chances of staying employed is to become an independent contractor, consultant, or business owner.

Here is an anecdote from my own career that illustrates this concept. When I was making the leap from employee to independent contractor (and subsequently business owner), my mother would wring her hands at the feast-or-famine nature of contracting. Under the misguided notion that a salaried job equals security, she would plead with me to get a "good job" with a steady paycheck and benefits.

Later, when half of California was laid off in the recession of the 1990s, she emphatically stated, "Thank God you own your own company!" (Okay, who are you, and what did you do with my mother?)

Many of my clients cut back on outsourcing at that time, but having multiple clients and multiple streams of income enabled me to survive the economic downturn (in contrast to staff employees who lost their entire incomes when they were laid off).

I'm not being negative so much as realistic when I say there is no such thing as job security. Even the members of the United Auto Workers union are finally realizing a company can't keep workers on payroll if there is no money to pay them, collective bargaining agreement or not.

Actually, let me clarify my earlier statement: there is no such thing as job security *when you work for someone else.*

I have job security because I know I will do whatever it takes to find enough work to pay the bills. Sometimes it takes long hours and a great deal of persistence and follow-through, but believe me, it pays off in the long run.

Cash reserves (to get you through the lean times) and flexibility (to respond to market changes) are important aspects of the consultant/ business owner route.

Advancing Your Career through Personal Branding

I recently went to a conference where attendees' name tags included the phrase, "Ask me about… [then an answer we provided when registering]."

While I initially just admired their clever way of giving attendees a way to break the ice when networking, my admiration soon shifted to a major career realization:

The whole concept of personal branding can be summarized by that simple phrase, "Ask me about…"

Before we look at some examples, let's define a few terms.

Branding vs. Positioning

According to BusinessDictionary.com, a *brand* is "a unique design, sign, symbol, word, or a combination of these, employed in creating an image that identifies a product and differentiates it from its competitors."

Think of Kleenex® brand facial tissue, Tide® brand detergent.

Companies spend billions of dollars a year advertising and building brand recognition so people will remember and buy their products.

It is interesting to note that in many cases, a name-brand product and a no-name generic product are the same product produced by the same manufacturer, just packaged differently. What matters is that consumers *perceive* that a brand name is better and therefore buy it, usually at a higher price than a non-branded generic equivalent.

Which brings us to the next key concept, *positioning*. One way to communicate to potential customers about a product or service is to compare it to a better-known product or service. "Stronger than steel," "Faster than FedEx®," "Cheaper than Walmart®" would be examples of positioning.

Notice that in each of these examples, the phrase contains some aspect of the product or company (quality, speed, price) and then a better-known product or company against which the item is positioned.

The Power of Branding and Positioning

Philip Morris originally launched the Marlboro brand in 1924 as a woman's cigarette, and advertising was based around how ladylike the cigarette was. When smoking was linked to lung cancer in the 1950s, Philip Morris repositioned Marlboro as a man's cigarette. Men at the time indicated that, while they would consider switching to a filtered cigarette, they were concerned about being seen smoking a cigarette marketed to women. So Philip Morris's advertising agency decided to use a lineup of manly figures in the ads, starting with a cowboy.

Within a year, Marlboro's market share rose from less than one percent to the fourth best-selling brand. This prompted Philip Morris to drop the rest of the lineup of manly figures and stick with the cowboy.

Personal Branding

One might say branding and positioning obviously apply to selling shoes or laundry soap, but what do they have to do with you?

That's where personal branding comes in. Just as a company creates a brand and promotes why people should buy their product or service, so should you create a personal brand and promote why people should buy *your* product or service.

Personal branding and proper positioning communicate why companies should buy your services and pay the rate or salary you want to be paid.

Responding to Market Changes

In their book *Built to Last: Successful Habits of Visionary Companies*, James Collins and Jerry Porras state that all the visionary companies they studied had one trait in common: they all had a history of responding to market changes while staying true to their core values.

Content Strategist Sharon Burton's rebranding story illustrates this beautifully:

> *"The whole reason I got into technical communications was not because I loved to write, it was because I loved being at the crossroads of people and technology and I could make a difference. That's why I do what I do. I realized what was true when I started is just as true today: I love being at the intersection of people and technology.*
>
> *"Unfortunately, writing online help topics just doesn't excite me anymore. But helping companies adopt a content strategy that gives people the information they need so they can go out and change the world? That excites me!*
>
> *"Industries change. These days companies need social media and webinars, YouTube videos and multichannel publishing. These are the areas in which companies are spending money, and they need help to do it right.*
>
> *"So the process of me rebranding wasn't just calling myself by a new title, it included reeducating myself and repositioning myself so I could effectively offer the services that companies need as the very ground beneath them changes."*

Alvin Toffler, an American writer known for his works discussing the digital revolution, takes the concept of reeducation a step further:

> *"The illiterate of the twenty-first century will not be those who cannot read and write, but those who cannot learn, unlearn and relearn."*

What Should People Ask You About?

How can you respond to market changes while staying true to your core values?

What do you do that you can promote as a specialized service for which you should be handsomely paid?

What should people ask *you* about?

Advancing Your Career through Progressive Information Disclosure

I had a fundamental, career-changing realization that I'd like to share with you.

But first, a question: what do the following have in common?

- TV or radio news
- Press releases
- Job interviews

Answer: progressive information disclosure (or lack thereof)

What is Progressive Information Disclosure?

I have been doing progressive information disclosure (PID) for most of my writing career, and newspaper editors have been doing it since the invention of paper.

So what is progressive information disclosure?

Wikipedia states that *progressive disclosure* is an interaction design technique that sequences information and actions across several screens to reduce the feeling of being overwhelmed for the user. In its most formal definition, progressive disclosure means to move complex and less frequently used options out of the main user interface and into secondary screens.

Similarly, progressive *information* disclosure:

- Enables you to provide the right information in the right place at the right time,

- Defers display of novice information, background information, concepts, etc., until the user needs and requests it, and

- Reduces complexity by revealing only the essentials for a current task, then reveals more information as users advance.

In printed media, newspapers support this brilliantly. So do well-written press releases.

- You skim the headlines to find a topic of interest.

- You read the first sentence to get the essence of what is being communicated.

- You can continue reading the first paragraph or two for more information.

- Then, if you are interested, you continue reading the rest of the piece.

This is progressive information disclosure; giving consumers the exact level and amount of information they want, when and where they want it.

Content consumers today are used to seeing "for more information" links on Facebook, in blog posts, etc. In fact, I'd say people who regularly consume online content expect to see them, and even get annoyed when they don't. We like progressive information disclosure—it enables us to receive just the right amount of information we want on any given topic.

This is especially true for people who (by choice or necessity) have to review large quantities of information in one sitting.

Also consider how many channels of information one might have to monitor. Personally, I sometimes feel overwhelmed keeping up with people I follow on Twitter, friends I follow on Facebook, the daily news, trade magazines, etc.

I need to be able to scan and quickly identify which topics I can live with just knowing that they happened (a headline), which topics I want to read a little more about (an interesting event), and which topics I really want to dig into (such as new development in my field).

Which brings me to my career-changing realization.

TMI!

I was driving to work one morning listening to NPR news and they played a segment about Nelson Mandela that was interesting…for the first minute or so. But then they kept providing more and more information (much of it repetitive).

Finally, I thought to myself, "TMI!" (too much information!) and I turned off the radio.

I'm so used to progressive information disclosure that I got frustrated at not having control over how much information was coming at me (well, more control than just turning off the radio).

Consider that the next generation of content consumers are used to communicating by text message, playing fast-paced video games, and watching fast-edited movies and music videos. Like me, they just don't have the patience to read long, boring reams of Too Much Information.

In the silence that ensued after I turned off the radio, I realized I've had that "TMI!" reaction before. In fact, it happens often.

The other day while interviewing a candidate by phone, I asked a simple question that required a yes/no answer. ("Do you have experience creating both printed and online documents from a single publishing database?")

The candidate, in turn, started talking about how long he's used databases, why single sourcing is a good idea, the projects he's done, etc.

Finally I had to interrupt him (TMI!) and say, "Thanks, but just answer the question, please."

If his answer had been "No," I could have gone on to the next question. If had been "Yes," I could have said, "OK, tell me about it," or I could have said, "Great, here's the next question." But he didn't give me that option—he just kept giving me information, information, information.

I suppose I could have simply waited for him to get to the point, but I just didn't have time.

People these days are constantly asked to do more with less (and managers have more direct reports than ever before), so time management is critical.

I know I'm not the only person to have such a reaction to too much information. A client of mine has a great response when one of her employees gives her TMI:

Manager: "Is the project done?"

Employee: "Well, first I had to do this, then I had to do that..."

Manager (interrupting): "Don't tell me about the labor pains. Just show me the baby."

TMI and Career Advancement

So how can you apply this idea about TMI to further your career?

First, actually listen to the questions you are asked, and answer accordingly. This applies in a job interview, in a meeting with your boss, etc.

Next, look for visual clues and feedback as to how much information each person wants. Start with just a sentence or two and pause. If the person wants more information, they'll tell you.

Pay attention to the types of information particular people want more or less of. For example, your boss might consistently want more information about project status and less information about, say, problems with co-workers. The saying, "know thy audience" absolutely applies to progressive information disclosure.

Be aware that the higher a person is on a company's organizational chart, the less time he/she has to spend with individuals. You might get a whole hour to pitch a proposal to your boss, but only five minutes to pitch that same idea to your company's CFO. By using progressive information disclosure in both your printed and verbal communication, you can address the information needs of multiple audiences.

Finally, realize that how much information is too much information varies from day to day (and even hour to hour) for any single person. Your spouse might ask you "How was your day?" at the end of each work day and normally be interested in an hour-long discussion. But if he or she is tired or hungry, you might cross the TMI threshold in thirty seconds. Part of communication is observing the reaction of the others involved and responding accordingly.

Monitoring and adjusting the amount of information you provide is a learned skill, one you may need to practice.

Progressive information disclosure is providing just the right amount of information where, when, and how the consumer wants it.

Sharpen your workplace PID skills and see if you don't start getting more praise, better assignments, and increase your standard of living.

Honing Your Workplace Negotiation Skills

For many people, the term "negotiating" brings to mind images of unpleasant haggling with a used car salesperson. But negotiation isn't something you do just when buying a large-ticket item like a washing machine or a car. Deciding what features will be implemented given the time on hand, getting your kids to clean their rooms before playing video games, even deciding what movie to watch on date night are all negotiations in one form or another.

What is Negotiation?

The *Merriam-Webster Dictionary* defines negotiating as "Conferring, discussing, or bargaining to reach agreement."

Dictionary.com defines negotiating as, "To attempt to come to an agreement on something through discussion and compromise."

I find these definitions lacking—they just don't capture the true spirit and goal of negotiation. So after reviewing my 25+ years of experience as a negotiator (first as a Systems Acquisition Officer in the Space Division of USAF, then as a staff and contract consultant, and finally as the owner of my own businesses), I created a better definition:

> *Negotiation is the art of giving up as little of what you have in order to get what you want.*

For what would you as an employee be negotiating?

- Your compensation
- Project scope
- Project deadlines

- Resources
- Head count
- Training
- Tools, etc.

What do you regularly give up in order to get what you want in the workplace?

Negotiation Basics

One negotiates to reach a common agreement. I believe all negotiations have to be either win-win or lose-lose to be considered "successful." Examples:

A sale: The buyer gets a product (or service) they wanted at a price they could afford, and the seller makes a reasonable profit.

A war: Both factions split the territory in dispute. Neither side is happy, but it's certainly better than fighting.

Win-lose is not "negotiating." When one side forces their terms on the other, there is no common agreement, no meeting in the middle. The other party may accept the offer because they have to, but they sure aren't going to like it, and they certainly are not going to give 100% if they feel they have been cheated.

What do you think a vendor will do who sells a service for less than what he or she considers a fair price?

What do you think customers will do if forced to pay more for something than they feel they should?

What do you think an employee will do if accepting a salary that is much lower than what he or she thinks is fair?

Before You Begin

The first thing to do before starting any negotiation is some homework. Decide before you begin what you would like to achieve. Decide what is a nice-to-have, what is a must-have, and at what point you will walk away from the negotiation if you are not getting what you want.

Don't try to decide these things *during* the negotiation. There is usually far too much stress or emotion in a negotiation, and you don't want to make a snap decision that you will later regret.

Chellie Campbell, author of *Zero to Zillionaire*, talks about doing business with "Your People." You recognize Your People when you meet them. They value your services and are happy to pay your rates for a quality product or service. They *want* to strike a deal that is good for both parties.

So the next step after doing your homework is to find Your People and negotiate with them.

At the Start

When opening a negotiation, don't just jump into price negotiations. Take time to get to know the person with whom you are negotiating, and for the person to get to know you. The person will be more open to negotiating if he or she feels you are "birds of a feather," so look for shared values and common ground.

Also, find out what is important to the other person and let the person know what is important to you. (More on this later.)

Opening Offers: Theirs

When possible, let the other side make the opening offer. That is the first insight you get into what they have in mind as a fair price, and you can determine if the deal is even worth pursuing.

For example, when a company comes to me looking for a contractor, I usually say, "Compensation can vary widely based on education and experience. Do you have a particular range in mind so I don't send anyone too expensive?"

If a client tells me they want someone for a ridiculously low amount, I assume they're telling me the truth—they really are looking for someone for $X/hour. In that case I don't even try to negotiate. I just say, "Sorry, there is no way I can find someone at that rate and still include a margin to cover my overhead."

But if their initial number is reasonable, you can ask to split the difference, or even just agree to their number if it is not too far from your own.

Opening Offers: Yours

There will be times when you will *have* to make the opening offer, such as stating your bill rate or salary expectations in an interview. I have a rule of thumb: the better the interview is going, the higher the number I quote when they ask my bill rate.

However, *I always add a qualifier in case I needed to back-pedal.* I say, "My *normal* bill rate is $X/hour…" and then watch their reaction.

If they accept my rate without hesitation, I make a mental note to raise my rates!

But if they react negatively, I can quickly add, "…but I'm flexible given that this is a long-term contract/given the state of the economy/etc."

AND—if they react negatively and I have to back-pedal, I also add, "What bill rate did you have in mind…?" This prompts them to reveal an opening bid, and again you can decide if the difference is so great that you should just walk away, or if it is close enough that you can meet in the middle, or if you should just accept their number.

Justifying Your Numbers

When estimating projects (no matter if you are an internal employee or external contractor), you must be able to show how you came up with your numbers.

The best way is to support your numbers with historical data. "The last time we did a project just like this it took…." If you can show exactly how you came up with your numbers, the negotiation will swing away from your hourly rate and onto the scope of the project.

Negotiating: Give and Take

Most people consider making and receiving concessions to be part of the negotiation process. So knowing the other person *expects* me to give up something as part of the negotiation, I always add things to my "wish list" that I am willing to negotiate away.

At the start of the negotiation you should ask the other party what is important to them. That way I can say, if you give me what is important to me, I'll do what I can to give you what is important to you.

When I do that, I find negotiating a deal is much closer to a dance than a tug-of-war.

Summary
- Negotiation is the art of giving up as little of what you have in order to get what you want.
- Find and negotiate with Your People.
- Take time to build rapport with the other party.
- Before you start, decide what you want, what you are willing to give up, and when to walk away.
- When possible, let the other party make the opening offer.

- Be able to back up your numbers and estimates.
- Go for a win-win agreement.

The Sky's the Limit

I once saw a comic strip of *Calvin and Hobbes* by Bill Watterson that describes the way I used to meet deadlines:

Hobbes: Do you have an idea for your story yet?

Calvin: No, I'm waiting for inspiration. You can't just turn on creativity like a faucet. You have to wait for the right mood.

Hobbes: What mood is that?

Calvin: Last-minute panic.

While waiting until the last minute can be effective motivation, it is far more comfortable (and profitable!) to plan your projects so that you can meet deadlines without killing yourself in the process.

That does not, however, mean you should only set small, comfortable targets.

I remember a conversation I had five years ago in which a friend was trying to convince me that I should be making five times what I was making. At the time I thought there was no way I could do that.

After that conversation, I started noticing every time I had negative success thoughts, like "I can't afford that, I'll never be rich," or "I wish I could have my own plane," (the unstated assumption being that I'd never have my own plane).

I stopped thinking I couldn't have or be those things, and starting asking myself *how* can I have or be those things?

I started to set higher goals, started researching how others did what I wanted to do, and started planning on how I could do the same.

You are the sole factor that determines whether or not you set and achieve your goals.

How successful do you want to be?

What Are You Waiting For?

Last year I had set aside a week to take an old friend from Ireland around New Orleans. We had a grand time eating and drinking, listening to jazz, visiting old plantations, and more. But at one point of the trip he asked if we could have a "serious" conversation, and he shared that he was dying of a rare but terminal disease.

I enjoyed the time we shared, and managed to hold it together for most of our visit, but I experienced deep, sobbing grief after we parted. (He had already come to terms with his mortality; I had not.)

During the trip he told me a story that I want to share with you:

"I was sitting in a pub a few months ago talking with a mate, and he asked me if I could live anywhere in the world, where would I live?

"I thought for a moment, then rattled off a list of requirements: I want to stay in this time zone so I can continue to service my clients (via Internet). I'd want someplace tropical, where the economy was prospering, where they had an interesting culture and great food, where people spoke English, and someplace where everyone has equal rights.

"My mate offered, 'South Africa.'

"I replied, Yes! I love South Africa! I've been there, the people are great, and it matches everything on my list!

"At that point my friend paused, looked me straight in the eye, and said, 'So what are you waiting for?'

"That stopped me dead in my tracks. I was about to stammer an answer, but realized I didn't have one. I had just stated if I

could live anywhere in the world I would live in South Africa, and there wasn't a single reason I could think of why not to go, except a voice in my head saying, 'What if...?' (fear).

"The next day I did my homework, found a real estate agent, and bought a plane ticket to South Africa!"

My friend's story reminded of three truisms:

- Everyone dies eventually, and you never know when your (or your friend's) last day will be.
- You can put off until someday things you want to do, only to realize in your golden years that "someday" came and went and you never followed your bliss.
- You don't need to have a terminal disease to live like you are dying (live each day to the fullest).

If you could live anywhere you wanted, do anything you wanted for a living, etc., what would you do?

So what are you waiting for?

About Making Money

One of the most valuable lessons I learned about making money and having stuff came from my father. While we couldn't afford *everything* I ever asked for (a pony when I was five years old and a speedboat when I was ten), my father always said, "If you earn half of the money, I'll put in the other half."

So as early as I can remember, I found ways to make money. As a child, I had chores around the house for which I earned an allowance. As a boy, I opened a lemonade stand in front of my house. Growing impatient for customers to come to me, I loaded my lemonade stand onto my red wagon and hit the road, going from construction site to construction site in the neighborhood, selling lemonade to the workers at each site.

From lemonade stands I started mowing lawns. Then I added edging to the service I offered as I could charge a little more for that. I babysat. Then got a paper route.

During summer vacation from school I worked as a construction laborer, I washed dishes in a restaurant, I went door-to-door selling stuff to raise funds for my Boy Scout troop.

My father was in the United States Marine Corps, and my mother was a school teacher. There were some interesting "conversations" in the house growing up with two Type A personalities wanting to be in charge. It was especially difficult when dad was deployed overseas and mom learned to be in charge, then dad would come home and want to assume head of household like he hadn't been gone. From this I learned that I don't have to be in control all the time. I step up when stepping up is required, and I hand the reins to someone else when it is their turn to lead. I truly believe that greatness includes knowing when to step back and let others contribute. (This especially applies to children and employees. Could I do it faster and better myself? Probably. But that helps neither the child nor the employee, and it leaves you doing all the work. Enough said.)

So the first lesson I learned was that I could have anything I wanted. All I had to do is earn money and get it.

How Can We Afford That?

Then came the problem of college.

I was a fairly good student and had the advantage of going to a private (Catholic) high school, but I knew that my parents couldn't afford to send me to an Ivy League school, and I just didn't want to go to a state university with 20,000 other students.

My solution: I applied for and received an Air Force ROTC scholarship to a college of my choice, in exchange for serving four years of active duty after I graduated.

That seemed like fair exchange, so I chose Tulane University in New Orleans and I majored in Computer Engineering.

My decision to apply for and land an ROTC scholarship changed my life. Not only was I able to attend a leading if-you-have-to-ask-you-can't-afford-it university, in New Orleans I gained an appreciation for good food, soulful music, and that quality of *joie de vivre* that New Orleanians possess—the ability to really enjoy life despite how much or how little you have in your checking account.

I've mentioned earlier how I went from being laid off from my sales engineer position to selling Ginsu knives, then becoming a contractor, then starting my own company. Then came the crash of 2008 and the years of clawing back from the brink of bankruptcy.

There were several books I read that really helped me get through those hard times that are worth mentioning.

The first was *Not Buying It: My Year Without Shopping* by Judith Levine. The book documented her year of not buying anything but necessities—including what she discovered was and was not a "necessity."

In the weeks after I burned through my savings and was just starting my technical writing contract, there were weeks where I barely had enough money for food. I learned how far one could stretch a dollar eating beans and rice. (Lucky for me I learned how to cook wickedly good red beans and rice and white bean soup while living in New Orleans. I could live on a pot of white bean soup for *days*.)

I learned what was and wasn't a necessity. For example: paper plates and paper towels? Not a necessity. I did without.

That lesson has carried over until today. Whenever I hear that voice in my head that says something like I *need* a 72" high-definition plasma TV, I'm reminded that "need" and "want" are two completely different things.

The next book that helped was *Rich Dad Poor Dad* by Robert Kiyosaki. The title comes from the fact that his real dad was a professor at University of Hawaii who would say things like, "We can't afford that," while his best friend's dad owned a string of convenience stores and would say things like, "*How* can we afford that?"

While I know my path in life is not real estate (as he suggests in the book), I did get the concept that it is far more enjoyable to figure out how to get stuff without paying a lot of money than it is to just slump into apathy and say, "I can't afford that."

One of the things I used to do in my darkest financial days was to go through a catalog and highlight everything I wanted (or alternately, go to a mall and look at everything I wanted), and then *not* buy it. I then added up how much everything would have cost and said, "Look how much money I saved!!!"

Robert Kiyosaki also states that the day you are generating more income from your investments than you are from your day job, you can finally quit your day job and "get out of the rat race."

That made me realize that at some point my income would hit a ceiling (based on how many hours I could work), so I needed to start looking for ways to generate passive income.

(Another Chellie affirmation: "My investments make me money even while I sleep!")

Get a Coach

It was about that time I heard Chellie Campbell speak at an event and bought her book *The Wealthy Spirit: Daily Affirmations for Financial Stress Reduction.*

Boy, did I need some of *that*!

In her book she says there are six keys to financial peace of mind:

Think positive. Like mind over matter, mind over money begins with believing you deserve it and can get it.

Send out ships. You can wait for your ship to come in, but if you don't send any out, it's going to be a long wait.

Count your money. Money is a game and you have to know the score. The money score will tell you how well you're doing at steps one and two.

Swim with dolphins. Being "in the swim" will depend largely on who you're swimming with. Find Your People and avoid sharks.

Survive the storms. You must weather interior storms as well as exterior ones. Persistence is key.

Seek balance and enlightenment. Only from your own perspective will you know when you have "enough."

After reading her book, I learned she offered an eight-week class based on these principles, and offered a money-back guarantee that you'd be making far more than the cost of the class. I have no trouble spending money to make money (especially when it comes with a money-back guarantee), so I said, "Sign me up!"

She's been my financial coach ever since.

There are times when you are so deep into whatever challenges you are facing that you "can't see the forest because of the trees." That's when you need a career or financial coach.

There is not a single winning professional athlete or team on the planet that doesn't have a coach. There's a reason for that!

Find a competent coach who will help you get results.

What Are Your Core Values?

So twice now personal values has come up in this book, the first in the section about responding to market changes while staying true to your core values, and above where Chellie refers to seeking balance and enlightenment.

Making money for money's sake is no fun. Ditto for leading a pauper's life.

I've met people who make tons of money, but they don't seem to enjoy it or do any good with it. They are like the seagulls in the movie *Finding Nemo* who go around saying, "Mine! Mine! Mine!Mine!Mine!"

I also know people who want to start a non-profit foundation that helps people, but they have no money to start a foundation *with*.

Money by itself isn't good or evil. It's what you *do* with it that shines light on your character.

So in an effort to "respond to market changes while staying true to your core values," I sat down one day (actually, I was on a flight home from Florida so sitting was kind of mandatory), and I wrote down my values, what I stood for with regards to starting my own company, why I want to make the money I want to make.

Here is an excerpt from what resulted from that exercise.

I began a project to update the company strategic plan. What started as writing just a sales lead generation program turned into a major codification of what the company stands for, where we are going, our purpose for existence.

> *Company Goal: An expanding, highly profitable staffing and education company with tons of cash reserves, happy, well-paid employees, and satisfied clients and candidates, with day-to-day activities handled by staff so the Founder can focus his time on public relations, marketing, pilot projects and social betterment projects.*

Note that our goal did not include (nor does it now) the purpose "to make money." Granted, a company needs to make money to exist as a company and individuals must make money to maintain a good standard of living. But history has shown that every time our focus strays from "providing good service" to "making money" we achieve neither.

I knew this datum about providing good service vs. making money was true at the time, but now (after twelve years and a few more gray hairs) I am convinced the datum is not just a smart observation, but a full-blown natural law. That is, we flourish and prosper when we strive towards our Goal, and crash and burn (quite spectacularly, I might add) when we stray from our Goal.

Re-Examining Our Goals

While writing down the company goal I realized there was a big whopping omission I can't believe I never spotted before: there was absolutely nothing in our company goal about employee development.

One of the reasons (if not *the* reason) I started my own company was to give myself and others an environment where individual incomes would be tied to production (not to some preset salary) and where we could take time off whenever needed to tend to our personal or family needs without the related arbitraries you find in most companies ("You only get so many days off," "You must be in the office from nine to five," etc.).

Considering that "wanting an arbitrary-free work environment" was one of the reasons I started my own company, to not even mention it in our company goal was a major omission.

And then I spotted another problem: I had never considered that funding charitable/social betterment programs was a reason for corporate existence. People who know me know I have a strong desire to support social betterment programs, and programs working to reverse global trends in crime, illiteracy, war, etc. In fact, another reason I started my own company was because it was one of the few ways I could help fund these programs to the level they needed to be funded. To leave social betterment off the list of goals was an omission equally egregious as leaving off employee development.

Next, I refocused the goal of the company from "profit" to "success" to mimic the successful actions of other, truly stellar companies I've been reading about of late in *Built to Last: Successful Habits of Visionary Companies* by James Collins and Jerry Porras.

Finally, given all the bad examples of what companies can do (witness the collapse of Enron, the sub-prime mortgage fiasco which lead to the credit crisis of 2008, etc.), I felt it was important to add one more goal: to help bring calmness and stability to people who are constantly bombarded by "crises" invented by the media and political establishments (not to mention the occasional actual crisis) by:

- Setting a good example of corporate ethics and sound financial practices
- Paying good wages for work well done
- Helping to calm individuals we work with (such as promptly servicing our customers, promptly paying our bills and subcontractors, etc.)
- Helping to calm people en mass through my writing and public speaking (on topics such as how to assert positive control over your career, your work environment, etc.)

Learning from Our Mistakes

Let me add that I am not claiming to be without fault in the area of financial management. I did not see the recession coming (and certainly not this bad a recession) and I ill prepared the company to weather a three-year economic downturn. As a result, the company came dangerously close to bankruptcy and I had to lay off some people I didn't want to let go.

But with hard work, tight belts, and sheer determination to make it go right, we have pulled the company back from the brink of collapse and are working to put our financial house in such good order as to be a shining example for others.

Bringing It All Together

Here are our goals and purposes for 2013 and beyond.

Company Goal:

An expanding, highly profitable services company with tons of cash reserves, happy, well-paid employees, and satisfied clients and candidates, with day-to-day activities handled by staff so the Founder can focus his time on public relations, marketing, pilot projects and social betterment projects.

Company Purposes:

- *To help our clients flourish and prosper by providing quality staffing, education, and consulting services*
- *To help our employees flourish and prosper by providing an arbitrary-free work environment that generously rewards production and supports personal enhancement*
- *To advance civilization as a whole by supporting global social betterment programs*

I believe we have good, basic purposes.

I hope you do as well.

Creating the Life You Want

As a final chapter in this book, I want to talk about one more thing: balancing what you want to do with what you need to do (such as familial obligations).

I don't have children, but I do have parents who are at the age (late 80s) where they not only need my help, but also want to spend more time with me. I, in return, want to spend more time with them (realizing that I'm not going to have them in my life forever).

My folks want me to move from Los Angeles (which I love) back to Jacksonville, FL (which I don't). I adore my parents and they have always been there for me, but I really don't want to move back to Jacksonville (for several reasons, not the least of which are the brutally humid summers).

So we compromised: I got an apartment there and split my time between LA, Jacksonville, and being on the road doing speaking gigs.

I didn't want to move into one of those bland cookie-cutter apartment complexes you see everywhere. One of the nice things about Jacksonville Beach (where my folks live) is that it is close to a lot of water—the Atlantic Ocean, the St. Johns River, the Intracoastal Waterway, etc.

So I told my dad to keep his eyes open for an apartment for rent somewhere near the water. In fact, I told him my ideal would be a mother-in-law's apartment behind a house on the Intracoastal Waterway, with a dock, and a kayak so I could go fishing.

Two weeks later he faxed me a classified ad from the local newspaper that said, "Waterfront apartment for rent."

I told him, "Get your digital camera and go take a look at it."

A few hours later he emailed me photos of a mother-in-law's apartment, behind a house, on the Intracoastal Waterway, with a dock… and a kayak!

I called him back and said, "Give them a check!"

The rent? $600/month (which, by then, was actually within my budget).

So now I am renting an oceanfront apartment in California and a waterfront apartment in Florida, all for less than most of my friends pay for their own house or apartments.

(And by the way, I am writing this last chapter from my friends' condo in Aspen, where I am pet sitting for three weeks while they are out of the country.)

The point to this tad long and self-promoting description of my life?

Because I went from being "this close" to bankruptcy and losing everything, to a lifestyle that enables me balance supporting and enjoying my family, while also making a living and enjoying some travel—while not spending a huge amount of money in the process.

If I can do it, so can you.

Mind you, this didn't happen overnight. It took me years of hard work and a fair amount of good luck.

But luck does favor the prepared, and the positive.

Another affirmation on my daily affirmation list: "I win often, and I win big!"

Years ago I realized at some point I would need to support my folks in their golden years, so I *specifically* chose a profession where I can work anywhere I have an Internet connection.

I visualized exactly the place I wanted to live, the way I wanted to live.

Sure, I thought positive, but I also sent out ships. Lots and lots of ships!

I never lost faith that I would win in the end, while simultaneously confronting the cold, brutal truth about the reality of my situation, no matter what that reality was.

I've made some mistakes in life, but I've learned from those mistakes, and in the end came out stronger because of them.

No matter where you are in your career—good, bad or indifferent—you have the power to change, to acknowledge your mistakes, learn from them, and press on.

Decide where you want to be one, two, or even five years from now.

Got that pictured? *Really* pictured?

Good.

Now go make it happen!

Recommended Reading

The Wealthy Spirit: Daily Affirmations for Financial Stress Reduction and *Zero to Zillionaire* by Chellie Campbell

Good to Great: Why Some Companies Make the Leap... and Others Don't by Jim Collins

Built to Last: Successful Habits of Visionary Companies by Jim Collins and Jerry Porras

Rich Dad, Poor Dad: What the Rich Teach Their Kids About Money—That the Poor and the Middle Class Do Not! by Robert Kiyosaki

The Richest Man In Babylon by George S. Clason

How To Outnegotiate Anyone (Even a Car Dealer!) by Leo Reilly

Get the Job: Optimize Your Resume for the Online Job Search by Pamela Paterson

About the Author

Jack Molisani started his career as a project officer in the Space Division of the U.S. Air Force, managing multi-million dollar development contracts. After finishing his military commitment, he worked various jobs in the private sector.

In the mid 1990s, he was laid off from his job with a leading technology company, an event that precipitated his getting out of the nine-to-five rat race once and for all.

Now a professional recruiter, Jack speaks at conferences and for professional organizations on how people can find work they love, make more money, and ultimately create the careers they've always wanted.